ELECTRONIC MAIL

ELECTRONIC MAIL

Mahendra Kumar Goel

RAJAT PUBLICATIONS
New Delhi

Electronic Mail
by *Mahendra Kumar Goel*

This edition is published by Rajat Publications
4740/23, Ansari Road Daryaganj,
New Delhi - 110002

ISBN: 978-81-7880-486-6

Edition 2026

Printed and bound in India

RAJAT
PUBLICATIONS

4740/23, Ansari Road, Daryaganj,
New Delhi- 110002 (India)
Mob:- +91-9811484973, +91-9811105389
E-mail: rajat_publication@yahoo.com

Preface

Electronic mail (e-mail) is a method of exchanging digital messages, designed primarily for human use. E-mail systems are based on a store-and-forward model in which e-mail computer server systems accept, forward, deliver and store messages on behalf of users, who only need to connect to the e-mail infrastructure, typically an e-mail server, with a network-enabled device for the duration of message submission or retrieval.

An electronic mail message consists of two components, the message header, and the message body, which is the e-mail's content. The message header contains control information, including, minimally, an originator's email address and one or more recipient addresses. Usually additional information is added, such as a subject header field.

People actively use e-mail to maintain core social networks, particularly when others live at a distance. The recent researches suggest that increase in the use of e-mail usage resulted in decrease in the use other modes of communication. With the introduction of chat messengers and video conference there are more e-ways to communicate.

The present book examines how electronic mail works, when it makes sense, and how to implement it. This up-to-date work describes all latest developments in this field.

Mahendra Kumar Goel

Contents

1

Introduction

The term "e-mail" applies both to the Internet e-mail system based on the Simple Mail Transfer Protocol (SMTP) and to X.400 systems, and to intranet systems allowing users within one organisation to e-mail each other. Often these workgroup collaboration organisations may use the Internet protocol or X.400 protocol for internal e-mail service. E-mail is often used to deliver bulk unsolicited messages, or "spam", but filter programmes exist which can automatically delete some of these.

Use of Spelling

Spelling of this term is disputed, and varies by field. While "e-mail" (with a hyphen) is used in journalism (such as by the CNN, BBC and New York Times), the computer industry primarily uses the spelling "email" (no hyphen). In particular, the original spelling is "email" (no hyphen), based on the technical roots of the term, as seen in the RFC documents for SMTP, POP and IMAP, which use "mail" or "email." "E-mail" is capitalised at the beginning of a sentence and in headings.

Origin of Email

E-mail predates the inception of the Internet, and was in

fact a crucial tool in creating the Internet. MIT first demonstrated the Compatible Time-Sharing System (CTSS) in 1961. It allowed multiple users to log into the IBM 7094 from remote dial-up terminals, and to store files online on disk. This new ability encouraged users to share information in new ways. E-mail started in 1965 as a way for multiple users of a time-sharing mainframe computer to communicate. Although the exact history is murky, among the first systems to have such a facility were SDC's Q32 and MIT's CTSS.

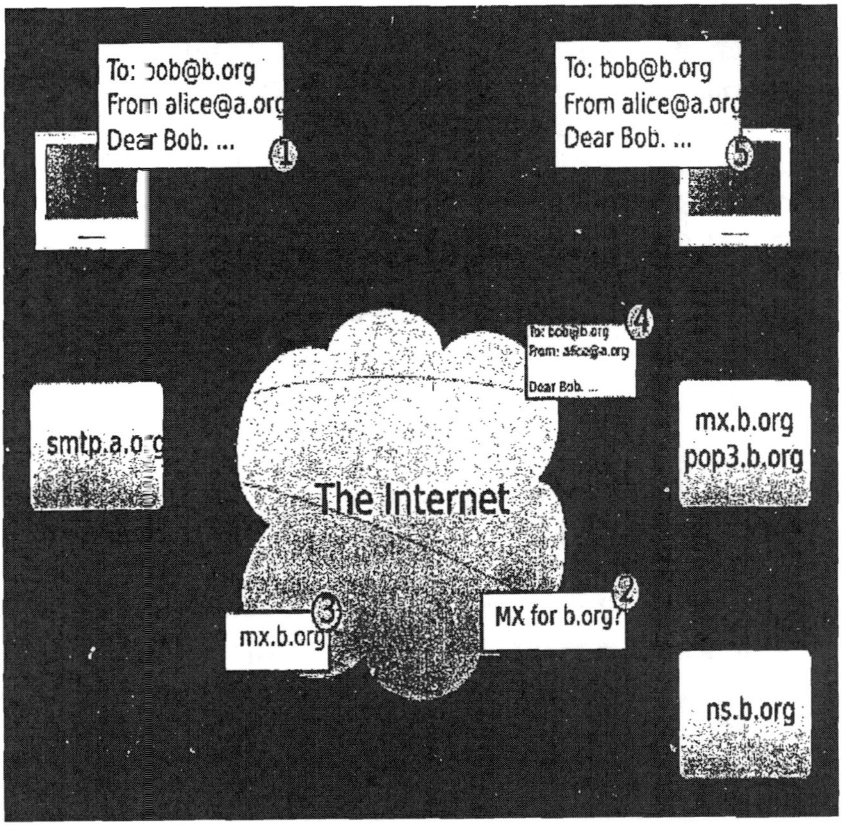

E-mail was quickly extended to become network e-mail, allowing users to pass messages between different computers by at least 1966 (it is possible the SAGE system had something similar some time before). The ARPANET computer network made a large contribution to the development of e-mail. There is one report that indicates experimental inter-system e-mail transfers on it shortly after its creation, in 1969. Ray Tomlinson initiated the use of the sign to separate the names of the user and their machine in 1971. The ARPANET significantly increased the popularity of e-mail, and it became the killer app of the ARPANET.

Workings

The diagram above shows a typical sequence of events that takes place when Alice composes a message using her mail user agent (MUA). She types in, or selects from an address book, the e-mail address of her correspondent. She hits the "send" button. Her MUA formats the message in Internet e-mail format and uses the Simple Mail Transfer Protocol (SMTP) to send the message to the local mail transfer agent (MTA), in this case smtp.a.org, run by Alice's Internet Service Provider (ISP).

The MTA looks at the destination address provided in the SMTP protocol (not from the message header), in this case bob@b.org. An Internet e-mail address is a string of the form localpart@ example domain.com, which is known as a Fully Qualified Domain Address (FQDA). The part before the @ sign is the local part of the address, often the username of the recipient, and the part after the @ sign is a domain name. The MTA looks up this domain name in the Domain Name System to find the mail exchange servers accepting messages for that domain.

The DNS server for the b.org domain, ns.b.org, responds with an MX record listing the mail exchange servers for that domain, in this case mx.b.org, a server run by Bob's ISP. smtp.a.org sends the message to mx.b.org using SMTP, which delivers it to the mailbox of the user bob. Bob presses the "get mail" button in his MUA, which picks up the message using the Post Office Protocol (POP3). This sequence of events applies to the majority of e-mail users. However, there are many alternative possibilities and complications to the e-mail system: Alice or Bob may use a client connected to a corporate e-mail system, such as IBM's Lotus Notes or Microsoft's Exchange.

These systems often have their own internal e-mail format and their clients typically communicate with the e-mail server using a vendor-specific, proprietary protocol. The server sends or receives e-mail via the Internet through the product's Internet mail gateway which also does any necessary reformatting. If Alice and Bob work for the same company, the entire transaction may happen completely within a single corporate e-mail system.

Alice may not have a MUA on her computer but instead may connect to a webmail service. Alice's computer may run its own MTA, so avoiding the transfer at step 1. Bob may pick up his e-mail in many ways, for example using the Internet Message Access Protocol, by logging into mx.b.org and reading it directly, or by using a webmail service.

Domains usually have several mail exchange servers so that they can continue to accept mail when the main mail exchange server is not available. E-mail messages are not secure if e-mail encryption is not used correctly. It used to be the case that many MTAs would accept messages for any recipient on the Internet and do their best to deliver them. Such MTAs are called open mail relays. This was important in the early days of the Internet when network connections were unreliable. If an MTA couldn't reach the destination, it could at least deliver it to a relay that was closer to the destination. The relay would have a better chance of delivering the message at a later time. However, this mechanism proved to be exploitable by people sending unsolicited bulk e-mail and as a consequence very few modern MTAs are open mail relays, and many MTAs will not accept messages from open mail relays because such messages are very likely to be spam.

Format of Internet e-mail

The format of Internet e-mail messages is defined in RFC 2822 and a series of RFCs, RFC 2045 through RFC 2049, collectively called Multipurpose Internet Mail Extensions (MIME). Although as of July 13, 2005 RFC 2822 is technically a proposed IETF standard and the MIME RFCs are draft IETF standards, these documents are the de facto standards for the format of Internet e-mail. Prior to the introduction of RFC 2822 in 2001 the format described by RFC 822 was the de facto standard for Internet e-mail for nearly two decades; it is still the official IETF standard. The IETF reserved the numbers 2821 and 2822 for the updated versions of RFC 821 (SMTP) and RFC 822, honoring the extreme importance of these two RFCs. RFC 822 was published in 1982 and based on the earlier RFC 733.

Internet e-mail messages consist of two major sections: Header—Structured into fields such as summary, sender, receiver, and other information about the e-mail Body—The message itself as unstructured text; sometimes containing a signature block at the end. The header is separated from the body by a blank line.

Message header

The message header consists of fields, usually including at least the following: From: The e-mail address, and optionally name, of the sender of the message To: The e-mail address[es], and optionally name[s], of the receiver[s] of the message

Subject: A brief summary of the contents of the message

Date: The local time and date when the message was written

Each header field has a name and a value. RFC 2822 specifies the precise syntax. Informally, the field name starts in the first character of a line, followed by a ":", followed by the value which is continued on non-null subsequent lines that have a space or tab as their first character. Field names and values are restricted to 7-bit ASCII characters. Non-ASCII values may be represented using MIME encoded words.

Note that the "To" field in the header is not necessarily related to the addresses to which the message is delivered. The actual delivery list is supplied in the SMTP protocol, not extracted from the header content. The "To" field is similar to the greeting at the top of a conventional letter which is delivered according to the address on the outer envelope. Also note that the "From" field does not have to be the real sender of the e-mail message. It is very easy to fake the "From" field and let a message seem to be from any mail address. It is possible to digitally sign e-mail, which is much harder to fake. Some Internet service providers do not relay e-mail claiming to come from a domain not hosted by them, but very few (if any) check to make sure that the person or even e-mail address named in the "From" field is the one associated with the connection. Some Internet service providers apply e-mail authentication systems to e-mail being sent through their MTA to allow other MTAs to detect forged spam that might apparently appear to be from them.

Other common header fields include :

— *Cc:* carbon copy
— *Bcc:* Blind Carbon Copy
— *Received:* Tracking information generated by mail servers that have previously handled a message
— *Content-Type:* Information about how the message has to be displayed, usually a MIME type
— *Reply-To:* Address that should be used to reply to the sender.
— *References:* Message-ID of the message that this is a reply to, and the message-id of this message, etc.
— *In-Reply-To:* Message-ID of the message that this is a reply to.
— *X-Face:* Small icon.

Many e-mail clients present "Bcc" (Blind carbon copy, recipients not visible in the "To" field) as a header field. Different protocol are used to deal with the "Bcc" field; at times the entire field is removed, whereas other times the field remains but the addresses therein are removed. Addresses added as "Bcc" are only added to the SMTP delivery list, and do not get included in the message data.

Body of the email

Content Transfer Encodings: E-mail was originally designed for 7-bit ASCII. Much e-mail software is 8-bit clean but must assume it will be communicating with 7-bit servers and mail readers. The MIME standard introduced character set specifiers and two content transfer encodings to enable transmission of non-ASCII data: quoted printable for mostly 7 bit content with a few characters outside that range and base 64 for arbitrary binary data. The 8BITMIME extension was introduced to allow transmission of mail without the need for these encodings but many mail transport agents still don't support it fully. For international character sets, Unicode is growing in popularity.

Plain Text and HTML: Both plain text and HTML are used to convey e-mail. While text is certain to be read by all users without problems, there is a perception that HTML-based e-mail has a higher aesthetic value. Advantages of HTML include the ability to include inline links and images, set apart previous messages in block quotes, wrap naturally on any display, use emphasis such as underlines and italics, and change font styles. HTML e-mail messages often include an automatically-generated plain text copy as well, for compatibility reasons. Disadvantages include the increased size of the email, privacy concerns about web bugs and that HTML email can be a vector for phishing attacks and the spread of malicious software.

Servers

Messages are exchanged between hosts using the Simple Mail Transfer Protocol with software programmes called mail transport agents. Users can download their messages from servers with standard protocol such as the POP or IMAP protocol, or, as is more likely in a large corporate environment, with a proprietary protocol specific to Lotus Notes or Microsoft Exchange Servers.

Mail can be stored either on the client, on the server side, or in both places. Standard formats for mailboxes include Maildir and mbox. Several prominent e-mail clients use their own proprietary format and require conversion software to transfer e-mail between them. When a message cannot be delivered, the recipient MTA must send a bounce message back to the sender, indicating the problem.

Filename Extensions

Most, but not all, e-mail clients save individual messages as separate files, or allow users to do so. Different applications save e-mail files with different filename extensions.

— *.eml* : This is the default e-mail extension for Mozilla Thunderbird and Windows Mail. It is used by Microsoft Outlook Express.

— *.emlx:* Used by Apple Mail.

— *.msg:* Used by Microsoft Office Outlook.

Use

In society

Many observers bemoan the rise of flaming in written communications. Flaming occurs when one person, usually upset at another person, sends the second person an angry and/or antagonistic message. Flaming is assumed to be more common today because of the ease and impersonality of e-mail communications: confrontations in person or via telephone require direct interaction, where social norms encourage civility, whereas typing an unhappy message to another person is an indirect interaction, so civility may be forgotten.

In business

E-mail was widely waccepted by the business community as the first broad electronic communication medium and was the first 'e-revolution' in Business communication. E-mail is very simple to understand and like postal mail, e-mail solves two basic problems of communication:

Pros

Problem of logistics: Much of the business world relies on communication between individuals who are physically distant from one another; organising and participating in an in-person meeting can be time-consuming and expensive. Email provides a near-instantaneous exchange of information at little cost. Teleconferencing bridges physical distance, but the logistics of gathering people together at the same time remains.

Problem of synchronisation: For real time communication, participants generally have to be working on the same schedule. They need to be at the same place at the same time and spend the same amount of time on the same information. E-mail allows each participant to decide when and how they will process the information.

Cons

Most business professionals today spend between 20% and 50% of their working time using e-mail : reading, ordering, sorting, 're-contextualising' fragmented information and of course writing emails. Use of e-mail is increasing, due to trends of globalisation-distribution of organisational divisions, outsourcing, among others. E-mail can lead to some well-known problems:

— *Loss of Context:* Information in context is much easier and faster to understand than unsorted fragments. Communicating in context is faster and more efficient.

— *Spam:* E-mail is a push-only medium: control of who receives information lies primarily with the sender. This can lead to an overflow of unwanted or irrelevant information.

— *Inconsistency:* E-mail can duplicate information. This may be a problem when a team is collaboratively working on documents.

Despite these disadvantages, and despite the availability

of other tools, e-mail-based communication is still the most widely used written medium in businesses.

CHALLENGES

Computer Viruses

The usefulness of e-mail is being threatened by three phenomena: spamming, phishing and e-mail worms. Spamming is unsolicited commercial e-mail. Because of the very low cost of sending e-mail, spammers can send hundreds of millions of e-mail messages each day over an inexpensive Internet connection. Hundreds of active spammers sending this volume of mail results in information overload for many computer users who receive tens or even hundreds of junk messages each day.

E-mail worms use e-mail as a way of replicating themselves into vulnerable computers. Although the first e-mail worm affected UNIX computers, the problem is most common today on the more popular Microsoft Windows operating system. The combination of spam and worm programmes results in users receiving a constant drizzle of junk e-mail, which reduces the usefulness of e-mail as a practical tool.

A number of anti-spam techniques mitigate the impact of spam. In the United States, U.S. Congress has also passed a law, the Can Spam Act of 2003, attempting to regulate such e-mail. Australia also has very strict spam laws restricting the sending of spam from an Australian ISP, but its impact has been minimal since most spam comes from regimes that seem reluctant to regulate the sending of spam.

e -mail Privacy Concerns

E-mail privacy, without some security precautions, can be

compromised because: e-mail messages are generally not encrypted; e-mail messages have to go through intermediate computers before reaching their destination, meaning it is relatively easy for others to intercept and read messages; many Internet Service Providers (ISP) store copies of your e-mail messages on their mail servers before they are delivered. The backups of these can remain up to several months on their server, even if you delete them in your mailbox; the Received: headers and other information in the e-mail can often identify the sender, preventing anonymous communication.

There are cryptography applications that can serve as a remedy to one or more of the above. For example, Virtual Private Networks or the Tor anonymity network can be used to encrypt traffic from the user machine to a safer network while GPG, PGP or S/MIME can be used for end-to-end message encryption, and SMTP STARTTLS or SMTP over Transport Layer Security/Secure Sockets Layer can be used to encrypt communications for a single mail hop between the SMTP client and the SMTP server.

Additionally, many mail user agents do not protect logins and passwords, making them easy to intercept by an attacker. Encrypted authentication schemes such as SASL prevent this. Finally, attached files share many of the same hazards as those found in peer-to-peer filesharing. Attached files may contain trojans or viruses.

2

E-mail Encryption

E-mail encryption refers to encryption, and often authentication, of e-mail messages. E-mail encryption usually relies on public-key cryptography.

Popular protocols for e-mail encryption include:

— S/MIME

— OpenPGP

— STARTTLS

Secure / Multipurpose Internet Mail Extensions (S/MIME)

S/MIME is a standard for public key encryption and signing of e-mail encapsulated in MIME. S/MIME was originally developed by RSA Data Security Inc. The original specification used the recently developed IETF MIME specification with the de facto industry standard PKCS #7 secure message format. Change control to S/MIME has since been vested in the IETF and the specification is now layered on Cryptographic Message Syntax, an IETF specification that is identical in most respects with PKCS #7.

Function of S/MIME

S/MIME provides the following cryptographic security

services for electronic messaging applications: authentication, message integrity and non-repudiation of origin and privacy and data security. S/MIME specifies the application/pkcs7-mime (smime-type "enveloped-data") type for data enveloping (encrypting): the whole MIME entity to be enveloped is encrypted and packed into an object which subsequently is inserted into an application/pkcs7-mime MIME entity. S/MIME functionality is built into the vast majority of modern e-mail software and interoperates between them.

S/MIME Certificates

Before S/MIME can be used in any of the above applications, one must obtain and install an individual key/certificate either from one's in-house certificate authority (CA) or from a public CA such as one of those listed below. Best practice is to use separate private keys (and associated certificates) for Signature and for Encryption, as this permits escrow of the encryption key without compromise to the non-repudiation property of the signature key. Encryption requires having the destination party's certificate on store. While it is technically possible to send a message encrypted without having one's own certificate to digitally sign, in practice, the S/MIME clients will require you install your own certificate before they allow encrypting to others.

A typical basic personal certificate verifies the owner's identity only in terms of binding them to an email address and does not verify the person's name or business. The latter, if needed, can be obtained through CAs that offer further verification (digital notary) services or managed PKI service.

Depending on the policy of the CA, your certificate and all its contents may be posted publicly for reference and verification. This makes your name and email address available for all to see and possibly search for. Other CAs only post serial numbers and revocation status, which does not include any of the personal information. The latter, at a minimum, is mandatory to uphold the integrity of the public key infrastructure.

Obstacles to Deploying S/MIME in Practice

Not all e-mail software handles S/MIME, resulting in a "smime.p7m" attachment that often confuses people. S/MIME is sometimes considered not properly suited for use via webmail clients. Though support can be hacked into a browser, some security practices require the private key to be kept accessible to the user but inaccessible from the webmail server, complicating the key webmail advantage of providing ubiquitous accessibility. This issue is not specific to S/MIME—any secure method of signing webmail requires a browser to execute code to produce the signature.

— Some organisations consider it acceptable for webmail servers to be "in on the secrets"; others don't. Some of the considerations are mentioned below regarding malware. Another argument is that servers often contain data that is confidential to the organisation anyway, so what difference does it make if additional data, such a private keys used for decryption, are also stored and used on such servers?

— Many make a distinction between private keys used for decryption and those used for digital signatures. They are far more likely to accept sharing of the former than the latter. This is especially true if the non-repudiation aspect of digital signatures is a concern (it may not be). There is fairly universal consensus that non-repudiation requires that a private key be under sole control of its owner during its entire lifecycle. Ergo, it's more likely to accept decryption done with webmail servers than digital signatures.

S/MIME is tailored for end to end security. Encryption will not only encrypt your messages, but also malware. Thus if your mail is scanned for malware anywhere but at the end points, such as your company's gateway, encryption will defeat the detector and successfully deliver the malware. Solutions:

— Perform malware scanning on end user stations after decryption.

— Store private keys on the gateway server so decryption can occur prior to the gateway malware scan.

— Use message content scanners specifically designed to check the content of encrypted messages in transit whilst preserving end-to-end signatures and encryption. Such solutions must contain built-in protection for both the private key used to decrypt the message, and for the temporarily decrypted contents.

Caveats

When a message is encrypted using S/MIME (or PKCS#7), the public key of each intended recipient is extracted from their certificates and those certificates are identified in the message by issuer and serial number. One of the consequences of this is that if a certificate is renewed, i.e. new certificate, same keypair, and the old certificate is deleted thinking it won't be needed any more, S/MIME clients will no longer be able to locate the decryption key to decrypt messages sent before the renewal, even though the key hasn't changed. In other words, deletion of expired certificates can have surprising consequences.

Even more generally, any messages that an S/MIME client stores in their encrypted form will not be decryptable if the certificate used for encryption has been deleted or otherwise not available, whether that certificate has expired or not. S/MIME signatures are usually done with what's called "detached signatures". The signature information is separate from the text being signed. The MIME type for this is multipart/signed with the second part having a MIME subtype of application/(x-)pkcs7-signature. Mailing list software is notorious for changing the textual part and thereby invalidating the signature.

Pretty Good Privacy (OpenPGP)

Pretty Good Privacy is a computer programme that provides cryptographic privacy and authentication. It was originally created by Philip Zimmermann in 1991. PGP and other similar products follow the OpenPGP standard (RFC 2440) for encrypting and decrypting data.

PGP Encryption Works

PGP encryption uses public-key cryptography and includes a system which binds the public keys to a user name. The first version of this system was generally known as a web of trust to contrast with the X.509 system which uses a hierarchical approach based on certificate authority and which was added to PGP implementations later. Current versions of PGP encryption include both alternatives through an automated key management server.

Encryption/decryption

PGP message encryption normally uses both asymmetric key encryption and symmetric key encryption algorithms. Commonly, when encrypting a message, the sender uses the public key half of the recipient's key pair to encrypt a symmetric cipher session key. That session key is used, in turn, to encrypt the plaintext of the message. There are several other operational modes, but these are less commonly used. The recipient of a PGP-encrypted message decrypts the session key using his private key.

Use of two ciphers in this way was chosen, despite higher complication, in part because of the very considerable difference in operating speed between asymmetric key and symmetric key ciphers. This approach also makes it easily possible to send the same encrypted message to two or more recipients. The entire encryption and decryption operations are completely automated in current PGP desktop versions. Many PGP users' public keys are available to all from the many PGP key servers around the world, most of which coordinate their records so as to act as mirror sites for each other.

Digital signatures

A similar strategy is used to detect whether a message has been altered since it was completed (the message integrity property), and whether it was actually sent by the person/entity claimed to be the sender (a digital signature). In PGP, it is used by default in conjunction with encryption, but can be applied to plaintext as well. The sender uses PGP to create a digital signature for the message with either the RSA or DSA signature algorithms. To do so, PGP computes a hash (also called a message digest) from the plaintext, and then creates the digital signature from that hash using the sender's private key.

The message recipient uses the sender's public key and the digital signature to recover the original message digest. He compares this message digest with the message digest he computed himself from the (recovered) plaintext. If the signature matches the received plaintext's message digest, it must be presumed (to a very high degree of confidence) that the message received has not been tampered with, either deliberately or accidentally. As well, since it was properly signed, it is very likely (to a very high degree of confidence) that the claimed sender actually did send it.

Web of trust mechanism

Both when encrypting messages and when verifying signatures, it is critical that the public key one uses to send messages to someone or some entity actually does 'belong' to the intended recipient. Simply downloading a public key from somewhere is not overwhelming assurance of that association; deliberate (or accidental) spoofing is possible. PGP has, from its first versions, always included provisions for distributing a user's public keys in an 'identity certificate' which is so constructed cryptographically that any tampering (or accidental garble) is readily detectable. But merely making a certificate effectively impossible to modify undetectably is also insufficient. It can prevent corruption only after the certificate has been created, not before.

Users must also ensure by some means that the public key in a certificate actually does belong to the person/ entity claiming it. From its first release, PGP products have included an internal certificate 'vetting scheme' to assist with this; it has been called a web of trust. A given public key (or more specifically, information binding a user name to a key) may be digitally signed by a third party user to attest to the association between someone (actually a user name) and the key. There are several levels of confidence which can be included in such signatures. Although many programmes read and write this information, few (if any) include this level of certification when calculating whether to trust a key.

The web of trust protocol was first described by Zimmermann in the manual for PGP version 2.0:

> As time goes on, you will accumulate keys from other people that you may want to designate as trusted introducers. Everyone else will each choose their own trusted introducers. And everyone will gradually accumulate and distribute with their key a collection of certifying signatures from other people, with the expectation that anyone receiving it will trust at least one or two of the signatures. This will cause the emergence of a decentralised fault-tolerant web of confidence for all public keys.

The web of trust mechanism has advantages over a centrally managed PKI scheme, but has not been universally used. Users have been willing to accept certificates and check their validity manually, or to simply accept them. The underlying problem has found no satisfactory solution.

Certificates

In the (more recent) OpenPGP specification, trust signatures can be used to support creation of certificate authorities. A trust signature indicates both that the key belongs to its claimed owner and that the owner of the key is trustworthy to sign other keys at one level below their own. A level 0 signature is comparable to a web of trust signature, since only the validity of the key is certified. A level 1 signature is similar to the trust one has in a certificate authority because a key signed to level 1 is able to issue an unlimited number of level 0 signatures. A level 2 signature is highly analogous to the trust assumption users must rely on whenever they use the default certificate authority list ; it allows the owner of the key to make other keys certificate authorities.

PGP versions have always included a way to cancel ('revoke') identity certificates. A lost or compromised private key will require this if communication security is to be retained by that user. This is, more or less, equivalent to the certificate revocation lists of centralised PKI schemes.

Recent PGP versions have also supported certificate expiration dates.

The problem of correctly identifying a public key as belonging to a particular user is not unique to PGP. All public key / private key cryptosystems have the same problem, if in slightly different guise, and no fully satisfactory solution is known. PGP's original scheme, at least, leaves the decision whether or not to use its endorsement/vetting system to the user, while most other PKI schemes do not, requiring instead that every certificate attested to by a central certificate authority be accepted as correct.

Security quality

To the best of publicly available information, there is no known method which will allow a person or group to break PGP encryption by cryptographic, or computational means. Early versions of PGP have been found to have theoretical vulnerabilities and so current versions are recommended. Indeed, in 1996, cryptographer Bruce Schneier characterised an early version as being "the closest you're likely to get to military-grade encryption." In contrast to security systems/protocols like SSL which only protect data in transit over a network, PGP encryption can also be used to protect data in long-term data storage such as disk files.

The cryptographic security of PGP encryption depends on the assumption that the algorithms used are unbreakable by direct cryptanalysis with current equipment and techniques. For instance, in the original version, the RSA algorithm was used to encrypt session keys; RSA's security depends upon the one-way function nature of mathematical integer factoring. New, now unknown, integer factorisation techniques might, therefore, make breaking RSA easier than now, or perhaps even trivially easy. However, it is generally presumed by informed observers that this is an intractable problem, and likely to remain so. Likewise, the secret key algorithm used in PGP version 2 was IDEA, which might, at some future time, be found to have a previously unsuspected cryptanalytic flaw.

Specific instances of current PGP, or IDEA, insecurities — if they exist — are not publicly known. As current versions of PGP have added additional encryption algorithms, the degree of their cryptographic vulnerability varies with the algorithm used. In practice, each of the algorithms in current use is not publicly known to have cryptanalytic weaknesses.

History of PGP

Phil Zimmermann created the first version of PGP encryption in 1991. The name, "Pretty Good Privacy", is humorously ironic and was inspired by the name of a grocery store, "Ralph's Pretty Good Grocery," featured in radio host Garrison Keillor's fictional town, Lake Wobegon. Of course, the irony is that PGP's security is not merely pretty good, but excellent. Zimmermann had been a long-time anti-nuclear activist, and created PGP encryption so that similarly inclined people might securely use BBSs and securely store messages and files. No license was required for its non-commercial use.

There was not even a nominal charge, and the complete source code was included with all copies. PGP found its way onto Usenet and from there onto the Internet, and it very rapidly acquired a considerable following around the world. Users and supporters included dissidents in totalitarian countries, civil libertarians in other parts of the world, and the 'free communications' activists who call themselves cypherpunks.

Criminal investigation

Shortly after its release, PGP encryption found its way outside the United States, and in February 1993 Zimmermann became the formal target of a criminal investigation by the US Government for "munitions export without a license". Cryptosystems using keys larger than 40 bits were then considered munitions within the definition of the US export regulations; PGP has never used keys smaller than 128 bits so it qualified at that time. Penalties for violation, if found guilty, were substantial. After several years, the investigation of Zimmermann was closed without filing criminal charges against him or anyone else.

Zimmermann challenged these regulations in a curious way. He published the entire source code of PGP in a hardback book, via MIT Press, which was distributed and sold widely. Anybody wishing to build their own copy of PGP could buy the $60 book, cut off the covers, separate the pages, scan them using an OCR programme, creating a set of source code text files. One could then build the application using the freely available GNU C Compiler. PGP would thus be available anywhere in the world. The claimed principle was simple: export of munitions-guns, bombs, planes, software was (and remains) restricted; but the export of books is protected by the First Amendment. The question was never tested in court in respect to PGP, but had been established by the Supreme Court in the Bernstein case.

US export regulations regarding cryptography remain in force, but were liberalised substantially throughout the late 1990s. Since 2000, compliance with the regulations is also much easier. PGP encryption no longer meets the definition of a non-exportable weapon, and can be exported internationally except to 7 specific countries and a named list of groups and individuals.

PGP 3

During this turmoil, Zimmermann's team worked on a new version of PGP encryption called PGP 3. This new version was to have considerable security improvements, including a new certificate structure which fixed small security flaws in the PGP 2.x certificates as well as permitting a certificate to include separate keys for signing and encryption. Furthermore, the experience with patent and export problems led them to eschew patents entirely. PGP 3 introduced use of the CAST-128 (a.k.a. CAST5) symmetric key algorithm, and the DSA and ElGamal asymmetric key algorithms, all of which were unencumbered by patents.

After the Federal criminal investigation ended in 1996, Zimmermann and his team started a company to produce new versions of PGP encryption. They merged with Viacrypt which then changed its name to PGP Incorporated. The newly combined Viacrypt/PGP team started work on new versions of PGP encryption based on the PGP 3 system. Unlike PGP 2, which was an exclusively command line programme, PGP 3 was designed from the start as a software library allowing users to work from a command line or inside a GUI environment. The original agreement between Viacrypt and the Zimmermann team had been that Viacrypt would have even-numbered versions and Zimmermann odd-numbered versions. Viacrypt, thus, created a new version (based on PGP 2) that they called PGP 4. To remove confusion about how it could be that PGP 3 was the successor to PGP 4, PGP 3 was renamed and released as PGP 5 in May 1997.

OpenPGP

Inside PGP Inc., there was still concern about patent issues. RSADSI was challenging the continuation of the Viacrypt

RSA license to the newly merged firm. The company adopted an informal internal standard called "Unencumbered PGP": "use no algorithm with licensing difficulties". Because of PGP encryption's importance worldwide, many wanted to write their own software that would interoperate with PGP 5. Zimmermann became convinced that an open standard for PGP encryption was critical for them and for the cryptographic community as a whole.

In July 1997, PGP Inc. proposed to the IETF that there be a standard called OpenPGP. They gave the IETF permission to use the name OpenPGP to describe this new standard as well as any programme that supported the standard. The IETF accepted the proposal and started the OpenPGP Working Group.

OpenPGP is on the Internet Standards Track; the current specification is RFC 2440 (July 1998). OpenPGP is still under active development and a follow-on to RFC 2440 was being actively finalized by the OpenPGP working group in 2006.

The Free Software Foundation has developed its own OpenPGP-compliant programme called GNU Privacy Guard (abbreviated GnuPG or GPG). GnuPG is freely available together with all source code under the GNU General Public License (GPL) and is maintained separate from several GUIs. Several other vendors have also developed OpenPGP-compliant software.

Network associates acquisition

In December, 1997 PGP Inc. was acquired by Network Associates, Inc. Zimmermann and the PGP team became NAI employees. NAI continued to pioneer export through software publishing, being the first company to have a legal export strategy by publishing source code. Under its aegis, the PGP team added disk encryption, desktop firewalls, intrusion detection, and IPsec VPNs to the PGP family. After the export regulation liberalisations of 2000 which no longer required publishing of source, NAI stopped releasing source code, over the PGP team's objection. There was consternation amongst PGP users worldwide at this and, inevitably, some conspiracy theories as well.

In early 2001, Zimmermann left NAI. He served as Chief Cryptographer for Hush Communications, who provide an OpenPGP-based email service, Hushmail. He has also worked with Veridis and other companies. In October, 2001, NAI announced that its PGP assets were for sale and that it was suspending further development of PGP encryption. The only remaining asset kept was the PGP E-Business Server (the original PGP Commandline version). In February 2002, NAI cancelled all support for PGP products, with the exception of the re-named commandline product. NAI continues to sell and support the product under the name McAfee E-Business Server.

Current Situation

In August 2002, several ex-PGP team members formed a new company, PGP Corporation, and bought the PGP assets (except for the command line version) from NAI. PGP Corporation is supporting existing PGP users and honoring NAI support contracts. Zimmermann now serves as a special advisor and consultant to PGP Corporation, as well as continuing to run his own consulting company. In 2003 PGP Corporation created a new server-based product offering called PGP Universal. In mid-2004, PGP Corporation shipped its own command line version called PGP Command Line, which integrates with the other PGP Encryption Platform applications. In 2005 PGP Corporation made its first acquisition-the German software company

Glueck and Kanja Technology AG, which is now PGP Deutschland AG. Since the 2002 purchase of NAI PGP assets, PGP Corporation has offered worldwide PGP technical support from their office in Draper, Utah.

PGP.com Encryption Applications

While originally used primarily for encrypting the contents of email messages and attachments from a desktop client, PGP products have been diversified since 2002 into a set of encryption applications which can be managed by an optional central policy server. PGP encryption applications include email and attachments, digital signatures, laptop full disk encryption, file and folder security, protection for IM sessions, batch file transfer encryption, and protection for files and folders stored on network servers and, more recently, HTTP traffic without TLS/OpenPGP.

The PGP Desktop 9.x application includes desktop email, digital signatures, IM security, laptop whole disk encryption, file and folder security, self decrypting archives, and secure shredding of deleted files. Capabilities are licensed in different ways depending on features required.

The PGP Universal 2.x management server handles centralised deployment, security policy, policy enforcement and reporting. It is used for automated email encryption in the gateway and manages PGP Desktop 9.x clients. It works with the PGP public keyserver-called the PGP Global Directory-to find recipient keys. It has the capability of delivering email securely when no recipient key is found via a secure HTTPS browser session.

With PGP Desktop 9.0 managed by PGP Universal Server 2.0, released in 2005, all PGP encryption applications are based on a new proxy-based architecture. These newer versions of PGP software eliminate the use of email plug-ins and insulate the user from changes to other desktop applications. All desktop and server operations are now based on security policies and operate in an automated fashion. The PGP Universal server automates the creation, management, and expiration of keys, sharing these keys among all PGP encryption applications. PGP Desktop 9.0 is available as a 32-bit application only, and therefore does not support 64-bit editions of Microsoft Windows including the 64-bit version of Windows Vista.

Hushmail

Hushmail is a web-based email service founded by Cliff Baltzley after leaving Ultimate Privacy. Hushmail offers PGP-encrypted e-mail, file storage, vanity domain service, and instant messaging (Hush Messenger). It was founded in May 1999 by Hush Communications (based in Vancouver, British Columbia, Canada, with offices in Dublin, Ireland; Delaware, United States; and Anguilla). The Hushmail.com servers are hosted in Vancouver. Hushmail uses OpenPGP standards and the source is available for download.

If public encryption keys are available to both recipient and sender (either both are Hushmail users or have uploaded PGP keys to the Hush keyserver), Hushmail can convey authenticated, encrypted messages in both directions. For recipients for whom no public key is available, Hushmail will allow a message to be encrypted by a password (with a password hint) and stored for pickup by the recipient, or the message can be sent in cleartext.

Hushmail has many added security features, such as hidden IP addresses in e-mail headers. Due to the small size of the free e-mail inbox, (2MB), and lack of IMAP or POP3 on free accounts, some computer users may prefer other e-mail solutions. Paid accounts have several hundred MB of storage as well as IMAP and POP3 access. To privacy advocates, it comes as the top recommended anonymous e-mail service by PC Magazine.

The Hushmail suite also includes a secure IM tool called Hush Messenger as well as web based key management tools. Users must trust, to a certain extent, that Hush's equipment or software are in honest hands, and always have been. Nevertheless, the design of the software, which is largely open for inspection, removes some of this need for trust. For example, barring unknown security holes, the Hush user's private decryption keys are not normally available to the operators of Hush's equipment.

Possible threats, such as demands from the legal system to reveal the content of traffic through the system, are not as imminent in Canada as they are in the United States.

GNU Privacy Guard

The GNU Privacy Guard (GnuPG or GPG) is a free software replacement for the PGP suite of cryptographic software, released under the GNU General Public License. It is a part of the Free Software Foundation's GNU software project, and has received major funding from the German government. GnuPG is completely compliant with RFC 2440, the IETF standard for OpenPGP. Current versions of PGP (and Veridis' Filecrypt) are interoperable with GnuPG and other OpenPGP-compliant systems. Although some older versions of PGP are also interoperable, not all features of newer software are supported by the older software.

GnuPG was initially developed by Werner Koch. Version 1.0.0 was released on September 7, 1999. The

German Federal Ministry of Economics and Technology funded the documentation and the port to Microsoft Windows in 2000. Because GnuPG is an OpenPGP standard compliant system, the history of OpenPGP is of importance. It was designed to interoperate with PGP, the email encryption protocol developed by Phil Zimmermann.

Version 2.0 was released November 13, 2006. The old stable 1.x branch, whose last version is 1.4.7 will be continued in parallel with the new GnuPG 2 series, because there were significant changes in the architecture of the programme which will not fit every purpose. GNU Privacy Assistant (GPA) a graphical user interface for GnuPG currently showing a list of public keys in a user's keyring

GnuPG is stable, production-quality software. It is frequently included in free operating systems, such as FreeBSD, OpenBSD, and NetBSD and nearly all distributions of GNU/Linux. GnuPG can be compiled for numerous operating systems. Cross compilation is not a trivial exercise, at least in part because security provisions vary with operating system and adapting to them is often tricky. High quality compilers should routinely produce executables which will interoperate correctly with other GnuPG implementations. Pre-compiled installations are available for popular operating systems including Microsoft Windows and Mac OS X.

Although the basic GnuPG programme has a command line interface, there exist various front-ends that provide it with a graphical user interface. For example, GnuPG encryption support has been integrated into KMail and Evolution, the graphical e-mail clients found in the most popular Linux desktops KDE and GNOME. They also offer graphical GnuPG front-ends (Seahorse for GNOME, KGPG for KDE). For Mac OS X, the Mac GPG project provides a number of Aqua front-ends for OS integration of encryption and key management as well as GnuPG installations via Installer packages. Instant messaging applications such as Psi and Fire can automatically secure messages when GnuPG is installed and configured. Web-based software such as Horde also makes use of it. The cross-platform plugin Enigmail provides GnuPG support for Mozilla Thunderbird and SeaMonkey.

In 2005, G10 Code and Intevation released Gpg4win, a software suite that includes GnuPG for Windows, WinPT, Gnu Privacy Assistant, and GnuPG plug-ins for Windows Explorer and Outlook. These tools are wrapped in a standard Windows installer, making it trivial for GnuPG to be installed and used on almost any recent Windows system.

Process

GnuPG encrypts messages using asymmetric keypairs individually generated by GnuPG users. The resulting public keys can be exchanged with other users in a variety of ways, such as Internet key servers. They must always be exchanged carefully to prevent identity spoofing by corrupting public key ? 'owner' identity correspondences. It is also possible to add a cryptographic digital signature to a message, so the message integrity and sender can be verified, if a particular correspondence relied upon has not been corrupted.

GnuPG does not use patented or otherwise restricted software or algorithms, including the IDEA encryption algorithm which has been present in PGP almost from the beginning. Instead, it uses a variety of other, non-patented algorithms such as CAST5, Triple DES, AES, Blowfish and Twofish. It is still possible to use IDEA in GnuPG by downloading a plugin for it, however this may require getting a license for some uses in some countries in which IDEA is patented.

GnuPG is a hybrid encryption software programme in that it uses a combination of conventional symmetric-key cryptography for speed, and public-key cryptography for ease of secure key exchange, typically by using the recipient's public key to encrypt a session key which is only used once. This mode of operation is part of the OpenPGP standard and has been part of PGP from its first version.

Problems

The OpenPGP standard specifies several methods of digitally signing messages. Due to an error in a change to GnuPG intended to make one of those methods more efficient, a security vulnerability was introduced. It affects only one method of digitally signing messages, only for some releases of GnuPG (1.0.2 through 1.2.3), and there were less than 1000 such keys listed on the key servers. Most people did not use this method, and were in any case discouraged from doing so, so the damage caused would appear to have been minimal.

Support for this method has been removed from GnuPG versions released after this discovery (1.2.4 and later). Two further vulnerabilities were discovered in early 2006; the first being that scripted uses of GnuPG for signature verification may result in false positives, the second that non-MIME messages were vulnerable to the injection of data which while not covered by the digital signature, would be reported as being part of the signed message. In both cases updated versions of GnuPG were made available at the time of the announcement.

GnuPG is a command-line based system, that is not written as an API which can be incorporated into other software. GPGME is an API wrapper around GnuPG which parses the output of GnuPG, and various graphical front-ends based on GPGME have been created. This currently requires an out-of-process call to the GnuPG executable for many GPGME API calls. Because GPGME makes use of a special GnuPG interface designed for machine use, a stable and maintainable API between the components is given. Possible security problems in an application do not propagate to the actual crypto code due to the process barrier.

X.509

In cryptography, X.509 is an ITU-T standard for public key infrastructure (PKI). X.509 specifies, amongst other things, standard formats for public key certificates and a certification path validation algorithm.

X.509 was initially issued in July 3, 1988 and was begun in association with the X.500 standard and assumed a strict hierarchical system of certificate authorities (CAs) for issuing the certificates. This contrasts with web of trust models, like PGP, where anyone (not just special CAs) may sign, and thus attest to the validity of others' key certificates. Version 3 of X.509 includes the flexibility to support other topologies like bridges and meshes. It can be used in a peer-to-peer, OpenPGP-like web of trust, but is rarely used that way as of 2004.

The X.500 system has never been fully implemented, and the IETF's Public-Key Infrastructure (X.509), or PKIX, working group has adapted the standard to the more flexible organisation of the Internet. In fact, the term X.509 certificate usually refers to the IETF's PKIX Certificate and CRL Profile of the X.509 v3 certificate standard, as specified in RFC 3280, commonly referred to as PKIX for Public Key Infrastructure (X.509).

Certificate

In the X.509 system, a CA issues a certificate binding a public key to a particular Distinguished Name in the X.500 tradition, or to an Alternative Name such as an e-mail address or a DNS-entry. An organisation's trusted root certificates can be distributed to all employees so that they can use the company PKI system. Browsers such as Internet Explorer, Netscape/Mozilla, Opera and Safari come with root certificates pre-installed, so SSL certificates from larger vendors who have paid for the privilege of being pre-installed will work instantly; in effect the browsers' owners determine which CAs are trusted third parties for the browsers' users.

Although these root certificates can be removed or disabled, users rarely do so. If pre-installed root certificates are removed on the Microsoft-platform, the operating-system re-installs them as soon as a web-site using the certificate is visited. As this mechanism relies on hash-values, pre-installed with the operating system, it is not even possible to determine which certificates are permanently trusted.

X.509 also includes standards for certificate revocation list (CRL) implementations, an often neglected aspect of PKI systems. The IETF-approved way of checking a certificate's validity is the Online Certificate Status Protocol (OCSP). Popular browsers like Internet Explorer and Firefox don't check for certificate revocation by default. The time lag for performing the checking could be one of the reasons.

The structure of a X.509 v3 digital certificate is as follows:

— Certificate

  — Version

- Serial Number
- Algorithm ID
- Issuer
- Validity
  - Not Before
  - Not After
- Subject
- Subject Public Key Info
  - Public Key Algorithm
  - Subject Public Key
- Issuer Unique Identifier (Optional)
- Subject Unique Identifier (Optional)
- Extensions (Optional)

— Certificate Signature Algorithm

— Certificate Signature

Issuer and subject unique identifiers were introduced in Version 2, Extensions in Version 3.

Certificate file extensions

Common filename extensions for X.509-certificates are:

— .CER - CER encoded certificate, sometimes sequence of certificates

— .DER - DER encoded certificate

— .PEM - (Privacy Enhanced Mail) Base64 encoded DER certificate, enclosed between "——BEGIN CERTIFICATE——" and "——END CERTIFICATE——"

— .P7B

— .P7C - PKCS#7 SignedData structure without data, just certificate(s) or CRL(s)

— .PFX

— .P12 - PKCS#12, may contain certificate(s) (public) and private keys (password protected)

PKCS #7 is a standard for signing or encrypting (officially called "enveloping") data. Since the certificate is needed to verify signed data, it is possible to include them in the SignedData structure. A.P7C-file is just a degenerated SignedData structure, without any data to sign.

PKCS #12 evolved from the PFX (Personal inFormation eXchange) standard and is used to exchange public and private objects in a single file. A.PEM-file may contain certificate(s) or private key(s), enclosed between the appropriate BEGIN/END-lines.

Security

In 2005, Arjen Lenstra and Benne de Weger demonstrated "how to use hash collisions to construct two X.509 certificates that contain identical signatures and that differ only in the public keys," achieved using a collision attack on the MD5 hash function.

Certificate authority

A certificate authority or certification authority (CA) is an entity which issues digital certificates for use by other parties. It is an example of a trusted third party. CAs are characteristic of many public key infrastructure (PKI) schemes. There are many commercial CAs that charge for their services. Institutions and governments may have their own CAs, and there are free CAs.

PUBLIC-KEY CRYPTOGRAPHY

Public key cryptography, also known as asymmetric cryptography, is a form of cryptography in which a user has a pair of cryptographic keys—a public key and a private key. The private key is kept secret, while the public key may be widely distributed. The keys are related mathematically, but the private key cannot be practically derived from the public key. A message encrypted with the public key can be decrypted only with the corresponding private key.

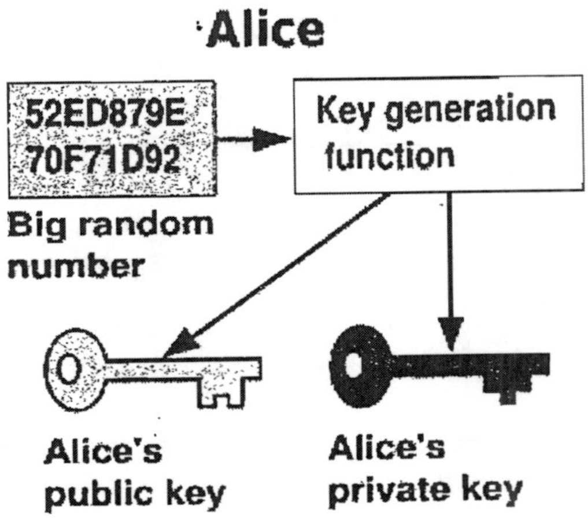

A big random number is used to make a public-key/private-key pair.

Conversely, secret key cryptography, also known as symmetric cryptography uses a single secret key for both encryption and decryption.

The two main branches of public key cryptography are:

— *Public key encryption:* a message encrypted with a recipient's public key cannot be decrypted by anyone except the recipient possessing the corresponding private key. This is used to ensure confidentiality.

— *Digital signatures*: a message signed with a sender's private key can be verified by anyone who has access to the sender's public key, thereby proving that the sender signed it and that the message has not been tampered with. This is used to ensure authenticity.

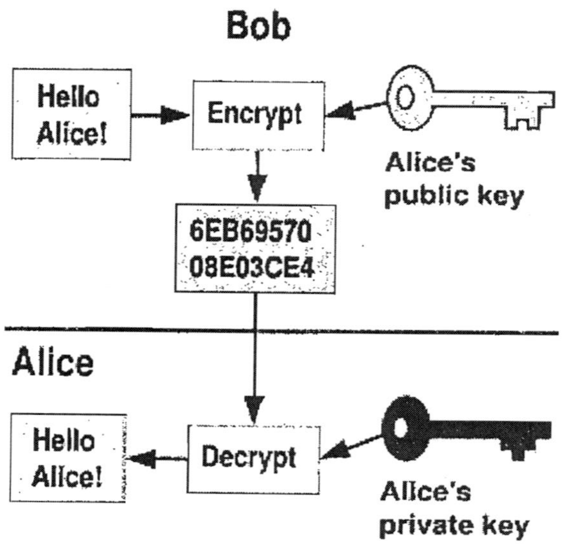

Anyone can encrypt using the public key, but only the holder of the private key can decrypt. Secrecy depends on the secrecy of the private key.

An analogy for public-key encryption is that of a locked mailbox with a mail slot. The mail slot is exposed and accessible to the public; its location (the street address) is in essence the public key. Anyone knowing the street address can go to the door and drop a written message through the slot; however, only the person who possesses the key can open the mailbox and read the message. An analogy for digital signatures is the sealing of an envelope with a personal wax seal. The message can be opened by anyone, but the presence of the seal authenticates the sender.

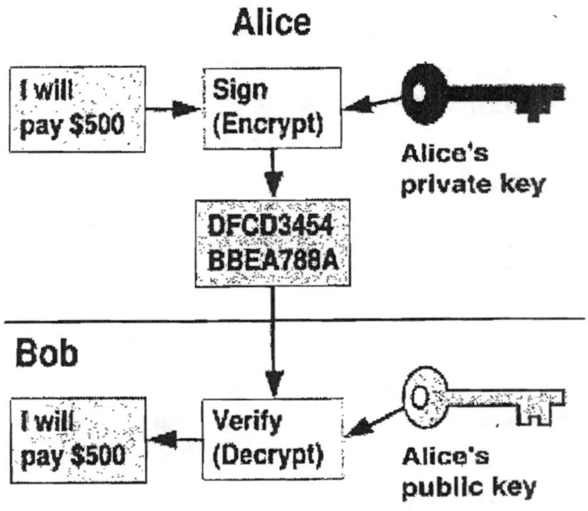

Using a private key to encrypt (thus signing) a message; anyone can check the signature using the public key. Validity depends on private key security.

A central problem for public-key cryptography is proving that a public key is authentic, and has not been tampered with or replaced by a malicious third party. The usual approach to this problem is to use a public-key infrastructure (PKI), in which one or more third parties, known as certificate authorities, certify ownership of key pairs. Another approach, used by PGP, is the "web of trust" method to ensure authenticity of key pairs.

Public key techniques are much more computationally intensive than purely symmetric algorithms. The judicious use of these techniques enables a wide variety of applications. In practice, public key cryptography is used in combination with secret-key methods for efficiency reasons. For encryption, the sender encrypts the message with a secret-key algorithm using a randomly generated key, and that random key is then encrypted with the recipient's public key. For digital signatures, the sender hashes the message (using a cryptographic hash function) and then signs the resulting "hash value". Before verifying the signature, the recipient also computes the hash of the message, and compares this hash value with the signed hash value to check that the message has not been tampered with.

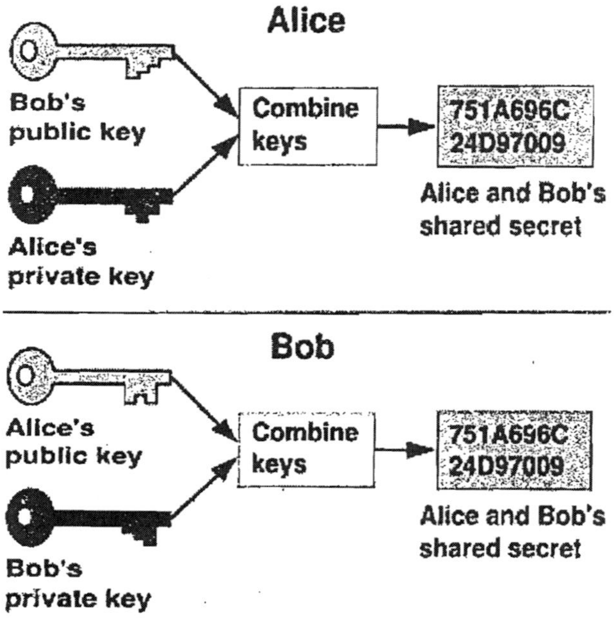

By combining your own private key with the other user's public key, you can calculate a shared secret that only the two of you know. The shared secret can be used as the key for a symmetric cipher.

For most of the history of cryptography, a key had to be kept absolutely secret and would be agreed upon beforehand using a secure, but non-cryptographic, method; for example, a face-to-face meeting or a trusted courier. There are a number of significant practical difficulties in this approach to distributing keys. Public-key cryptography was invented to address these drawbacks—with public-key cryptography, users can communicate securely over an insecure channel without having to agree upon a shared key beforehand.

In 1874, a book by William Stanley Jevons described the relationship of one-way functions to cryptography and went on to discuss specifically the factorisation problem used to create the trapdoor function in the RSA system. In July 1996, one observer commented on the Jevons book in this way:

> In his book The Principles of Science: A Treatise on Logic and Scientific Method, written and published in the 1890s, William S. Jevons observed that there are many situations where the 'direct' operation is relatively easy, but the 'inverse' operation is significantly more difficult. One example mentioned briefly is that enciphering (encryption) is easy while deciphering (decryption) is not. In the same section of Chapter 7: Introduction titled 'Induction an Inverse Operation', much more attention is devoted to the principle that multiplication of integers is easy, but finding the (prime) factors of the product is much harder. Thus, Jevons anticipated a key feature of the RSA Algorithm for public key cryptography, though he certainly did not invent the concept of public key cryptography.

The first invention of asymmetric key algorithms was by James H. Ellis, Clifford Cocks, and Malcolm Williamson at GCHQ in the UK in the early 1970s; these inventions were what later become known as Diffie-Hellman key exchange, and a special case of RSA. The GCHQ cryptographers referred to the technique as "non-secret encryption". These inventions were not publicly disclosed at the time, and the fact that they had been developed was kept secret until 1997.

An asymmetric-key cryptosystem was published in 1976 by Whitfield Diffie and Martin Hellman, who, influenced by Ralph Merkle's work on public-key distribution, disclosed a method of public-key agreement. This method of exponential-key exchange, which came to be known as Diffie-Hellman key exchange, was the first published practical method for establishing a shared secret-key over an unprotected communications channel without using a prior shared secret. Merkle's public-key-agreement technique became known as Merkle's Puzzles, and was published in 1978.

A generalisation of the Cocks method was reinvented in 1977 by Rivest, Shamir and Adleman, all then at MIT. The latter authors published their work in 1978, and the algorithm appropriately came to be known as RSA. RSA uses exponentiation modulo a product of two large primes to encrypt and decrypt, performing both public key encryption and public key digital signature, and its security is connected to the presumed difficulty of factoring large integers, a problem for which there is no known efficient (i.e., practicably fast) general technique.

Since the 1970s, a large number and variety of encryption, digital signature, key agreement, and other techniques have been developed in the field of public-key cryptography. The ElGamal cryptosystem (invented by Taher ElGamal then of Netscape) relies on the (similar, and related) difficulty of the discrete logarithm problem, as does the closely related DSA developed by the NSA and NIST. The introduction of elliptic curve cryptography by Neal Koblitz in the mid 1980s has yielded a new family of analogous public-key algorithms. Although mathematically more complex, elliptic curves appear to provide a more efficient way to leverage the discrete logarithm problem, particularly with respect to key size.

Cryptographic Algorithms

There is nothing especially more secure about asymmetric key algorithms than symmetric key algorithms. There are popular ones and unpopular ones. There are broken ones and ones that are, for now, not broken. Unfortunately, popularity is not a reliable indicator of security. Some algorithms have security proofs with various properties and of varying quality. Many proofs claim that breaking an algorithm, with respect to some well-defined security goals, is equivalent to solving one of the more popular mathematical problems that are presumed to be intractable, like factoring the product of two large primes or finding discrete logarithms. Some proofs have also been shown to be flawed. None of these algorithms can be proved secure in as absolute a sense as the one-time pad has. As with all cryptographic algorithms, these algorithms must be chosen and used with care.

The most obvious application of a public key encryption system is confidentiality; a message which a sender encrypts using the recipient's public key can only be decrypted by the recipient's paired private key.

Public-key digital signature algorithms can be used for sender authentication and non-repudiation. For instance, a user can encrypt a message with his own private key and send it. If another user can successfully decrypt it using the corresponding public key, this provides assurance that the first user (and no other) sent it. In practice, a cryptographic hash value of the message is calculated, encrypted with the private key and sent along with the message (resulting in a cryptographic signature of the message). The receiver can then verify message integrity and origin by calculating the hash value of the received message and comparing it against the decoded signature (the original hash). If the hash from the sender and the hash on the receiver side do not match, then the received message is not identical to the message which the sender "signed", or the sender's identity is wrong.

To achieve authentication, non-repudiation, and confidentiality, the sender would first encrypt the message using his private key, then a second encryption is performed using the recipient's public key. These characteristics are useful for many other, sometimes surprising, applications, like digital cash, password-authenticated key agreement, multi-party key agreement, etc.

Practical Considerations

An analogy which can be used to understand the advantages of an asymmetric system is to imagine two people, Alice and Bob, sending a secret message through the public mail. In this example, Alice wants to send a secret message to Bob, and expects a secret reply from Bob.

With a symmetric key system, Alice first puts the secret message in a box, and locks the box using a padlock to which she has a key. She then sends the box to Bob through regular mail. When Bob receives the box, he uses an identical copy of Alice's key (which he has somehow obtained previously, maybe by a face-to-face meeting) to open the box, and reads the message. Bob can then use the same padlock to send his secret reply.

In an asymmetric key system, Bob and Alice have separate padlocks. First, Alice asks Bob to send his open padlock to her through regular mail, keeping his key to himself. When Alice receives it she uses it to lock a box containing her message, and sends the locked box to Bob. Bob can then unlock the box with his key and read the message from Alice. To reply, Bob must similarly get Alice's open padlock to lock the box before sending it back to her.

The critical advantage in an asymmetric key system is that Bob and Alice never need to send a copy of their keys to each other. This prevents a third party (perhaps, in the example, a corrupt postal worker) from copying a key while it is in transit, allowing said third party to spy on all future messages sent between Alice and Bob. So in the public key scenario, Alice and Bob need not trust the postal service as much. In addition, if Bob were careless and allow someone else to copy his key, Alice's messages to Bob would be compromised, but Alice's messages to other people would remain secret, since the other people would be providing different padlocks for Alice to use.

Actual algorithms-two linked keys

Not all asymmetric key algorithms operate in precisely this fashion. The most common ones have the property that Alice and Bob each own two keys, one for encryption and one for decryption. In a secure asymmetric key encryption scheme, the decryption key should not be deducible from the encryption key. This is known as public-key encryption, since the encryption key can be published without compromising the security of encrypted messages. In the analogy above, Bob might publish instructions on how to make a lock ("public key"), but the lock is such that it is impossible (so far as is known) to deduce from these instructions how to make a key which will open that lock ("private key"). Those wishing to send messages to Bob use the public key to encrypt the message; Bob uses his private key to decrypt it.

Of course, there is a possibility that someone could "pick" Bob's or Alice's lock. Among symmetric key encryption algorithms, only the one-time pad can be proven to be secure against any adversary, no matter how much computing power is available. Unfortunately, there is no public-key scheme with this property, since all public-key schemes are susceptible to brute force key search attack. Such attacks are impractical if the amount of computation needed to succeed (termed 'work factor' by Shannon) is out of reach of potential attackers. The work factor can be increased by simply choosing a longer key. Other attacks may be more efficient, and some are known for some public key encryption algorithms. Both RSA and ElGamal have known attacks which are much faster than the brute force approach. Such estimates have changed both with the decreasing cost of computer power, and new mathematical discoveries.

In practice, these insecurities can be avoided by choosing key sizes large enough that the best known attack would take so long that it is not worth any adversary's time and money to break the code. For example, if an estimate of how long it takes to break an encryption scheme is one thousand years, and it were used to encrypt your credit card details, they would be safe enough, since the time needed to decrypt the details will be rather longer than the useful life of those details, which expire after a few years. Typically, the key size needed is much longer for public key algorithms than for symmetric key algorithms.

Major weaknesses have been found for several formerly promising asymmetric key algorithms. The 'knapsack packing' algorithm was found to be insecure when a new attack was found. Recently, some attacks based on careful measurements of the exact amount of time it takes known hardware to encrypt plain text have been used to simplify the search for likely decryption keys. Thus, mere use of asymmetric key algorithms does not ensure security; it is an area of active research to discover and protect against new attacks.

Another potential security vulnerability in using asymmetric keys is the possibility of a man in the middle attack, in which communication of public keys is intercepted by a third party and modified to provide different public keys instead. Encrypted messages and responses must also be intercepted, decrypted and re-encrypted by the attacker using the correct public keys for different communication segments in all instances to avoid suspicion. This attack may seem to be difficult to implement in practice, but it's not impossible when using insecure media. A malicious staff member at Alice or Bob's ISP might find it outright easy.

One approach to prevent such attacks is the use of a certificate authority, a trusted third party who is responsible for verifying the identity of a user of the system and issuing a digital certificate, which is a signed block of data stating that this public key belongs to that person, company or other entity. This approach also has weaknesses. For example, the certificate authority must be trusted to have properly checked the identity of the key-holder and the correctness of the public key when it issues a certificate, and has been correctly set up at communication participants before it can be used.

An attacker who could subvert the certificate authority into issuing a certificate for a bogus public key could then mount a man in the middle attack as easily as if the certificate scheme were not used at all. Despite its problems, this approach is widely used; examples include SSL and its successor, TLS, which are commonly used to provide security in web browsers, for example, to securely send credit card details to an online store.

Computational cost

Most public key algorithms are relatively computationally costly in comparison with many symmetric key algorithms of apparently equivalent security. This has important implications for their practical use. Most are used in hybrid cryptosystems for reasons of efficiency; in such a cryptosystem, a shared secret key ("session key") is generated by one party and this much briefer session key is then encrypted by each recipient's public key. Each recipient uses the corresponding private key to decrypt the session key. Once all parties have obtained the session key they can use a much faster symmetric algorithm to encrypt and decrypt messages.

Associating public keys with identities

The binding between a public key and its 'owner' must be correct, lest the algorithm function perfectly and yet be entirely insecure in practice. As with most cryptography, the protocols used to establish and verify this binding are critically important. Associating a public key with its owner is typically done by protocols implementing a public key infrastructure; these allow the validity of the association to be formally verified by reference to a trusted third party, either in the form of a hierarchical certificate authority (e.g., X.509), a local trust model (e.g., SPKI), or a web of trust scheme.

Whatever the cryptographic assurance of the protocols themselves, the association between a public key and its owner is ultimately a matter of subjective judgement on the part of the trusted third party, since the key is a mathematical entity whilst the owner, and the connection between owner and key, are not. For this reason, the formalism of a public key infrastructure must provide for explicit statements of the policy followed when making this judgement. For example, the complex and never fully implemented X.509 standard allows a certificate authority to identify its policy by means of an object identifier which functions as an index into a catalogue of registered policies. Policies may exist for many different purposes, ranging from anonymity to military classification.

Relation to real world events

A public key will be known to a large and, in practice,

unknown set of users. All events requiring revocation or replacement of a public key can take a long time to take full effect with all who must be informed (i.e. all those users who possess that key). For this reason, systems which must react to events in real time should not use public-key encryption without taking great care. There are four issues of interest:

A malicious (or erroneous) revocation of some, or all, of the keys in the system is likely, in the second case, certain, to cause a complete failure of the system. If public keys can be revoked individually, this is a possibility. However, there are design approaches which can reduce the practical chance of this occurring. For example, by means of certificates we can create what is called a "compound principal"; one such principal could be "Alice and Bob have Revoke Authority". Now only Alice and Bob (in concert) can revoke a key, and neither Alice nor Bob can revoke keys alone. However, revoking a key now requires both Alice and Bob to be available, and this creates a problem of reliability.

In concrete terms, from a security point of view, there is now a single point of failure in the public key revocation system. A successful Denial of Service attack against either Alice or Bob (or both) will block a required revocation. In fact, any partition of authority between Alice and Bob will have this effect, regardless of how it comes about.

Because the principal having revocation authority for keys is very powerful, the mechanisms used to control it should involve both as many participants as possible (to guard against malicious attacks of this type), while at the same time as few as possible (to ensure that a key can be revoked without dangerous delay). Public key certificates which include an expiry date are unsatisfactory in that the expiry date may not correspond with a real world revocation need, but at least such certificates need not all be tracked down system wide, nor must all users be in constant contact with the system at all times.

After a key has been revoked, or when a new user is added to a system, a new key must be distributed in some predetermined manner. Assume that Carol's key has been revoked (e.g. automatically by exceeding its use-before date, or less so, because of a compromise of Carol's matching private key). Until a new key has been distributed, Carol is effectively out of contact. No one will be able to send her messages without violating system protocols (i.e. without a valid public key, no one can encrypt messages to her), and messages from her cannot be signed for the same reason. Or, in other words, the "part of the system" controlled by Carol is essentially unavailable. Security requirements have been ranked higher than system availability in such designs.

One could leave the authority to create new keys (and certify them) and the authority to revoke them in the hands of each user, and the original PGP design did so, but this raises problems of user understanding and operation. For security reasons, this approach has considerable difficulties; if nothing else, some users will be forgetful or inattentive or confused. On one hand, a public key certificate revoking message should be spread as fast as possible while, on the other hand, (parts of) the system might be rendered inoperable before a new key can be installed. The time window can obviously be reduced to zero by always issuing the new key together with the certificate that revokes the old one, but this requires co-location of both authority to revoke and to generate new keys.

It is most likely a system-wide failure if the (possibly combined) principal that issues new keys fails by issuing keys improperly. It is an instance of a common mutual exclusion; a design can make the reliability of a system high, but only at the cost of system availability, and vice versa.

Notification of a key certificate revocation must be spread to all those who might potentially hold it, and as rapidly as possible. There are two means of spreading information (e.g., a key revocation here) in a distributed system: either the information is pushed to users from a central point(s), or it is pulled from a central point(s) to end users.

Pushing the information is the simplest solution in that a message is sent to all participants. However, there is no way of knowing that all participants will actually receive the message, and if the number of participants is large and some of their physical or network distance great, the probability of complete success (which is, ideally, required for system security) will be rather low. In a partially updated state, the system is particularly vulnerable to denial of service attacks as security has been breached, and a vulnerability window will continue to exist as long as some users have not 'gotten the word'. In other words, pushing certificate revocation messages is neither easy to secure nor very reliable.

The alternative to pushing is pulling. In the extreme, all certificates contain all the keys needed to verify that the public key of interest (i.e. the one belonging to the user to whom one wishes to send a message, or whose signature is to be checked) is still valid. In this case, at least some use of the system will be blocked if a user cannot reach the verification service (i.e. one of those systems which can establish the current validity of another user's key). Again, such a system design can be made as reliable as one wishes, at the cost of lowering security (the more servers to check for the possibility of a key revocation, the longer the window of vulnerability).

Another trade-off is to use a somewhat less reliable, but more secure, verification service but to include an expiry date for each of the verification sources. How long this timeout should be is a decision which embodies a trade-off between availability and security that will have to be decided in advance, at system design time.

Assume that the principal authorised to revoke a key has decided that a certain key must be revoked. In most cases this happens after the fact; for instance, it becomes known that at some time in the past an event occurred that endangered a private key. Let us denote the time at which it is decided that the compromise occurred with T.

Such a compromise has two implications. Messages encrypted with the matching public key (now or in the past) can no longer be assumed to be secret. Second, signatures made with the no longer trusted to be actually private key after time T, can no longer be assumed to be authentic without additional information about who, where, when, etc of the events leading up to digital signature. These will not always be available, and so all such digital signatures will be less than credible.

Loss of secrecy and/or authenticity, even for a single user, has system-wide security implications, and a strategy for recovery must thus be established. Such a strategy will determine who has authority and under what conditions to revoke a public key certificate, how to spread the revocation, but also, ideally, how to deal with all messages signed with the key since time T (which will rarely be known precisely). Messages sent to that user must be considered compromised as well, no matter when they were sent.

3

HTML E-mail

HTML e-mail is the use of a subset of HTML (often ill-defined) to provide formatting and semantic markup capabilities in e-mail that are not available with plain text. HTML mail allows the sender to properly express quotations (as in inline replying), headings, bulleted lists, emphasized text, subscripts and superscripts, and other visual and typographic cues to improve the readability and aesthetics of the message. Long URLs can be linked to without being broken into multiple pieces, and text is wrapped to fit the width of the user agent's viewport, instead of uniformly breaking each line at 78 characters (defined in RFC 2822, which was necessary on older data terminals). It allows in-line inclusion of tables, diagrams, or mathematical formulae as images, which are otherwise difficult to convey (typically using ASCII art).

Since its conception, a number of people have vocally opposed all HTML e-mail (and even MIME itself), for a variety of reasons. While still considered inappropriate in many news group postings and mailing lists, its adoption for personal and business mail has only increased over time. Some of those who strongly opposed it when it first came out now see it as mostly harmless.

Compatibility Issues

According to surveys by online marketing companies, the vast majority of Internet users can access HTML mail, and a smaller number, though still the majority, prefer it over plain text. As HTML mail is more complex than plain text, however, it is also more prone to compatibility issues and problems with rendering consistently across platforms and software. Some popular e-mail clients do not render consistently with W3C specifications, and many HTML e-mails are not compliant, either, which may cause rendering or delivery problems, especially for users of MSN or Hotmail.

In particular, the <head> tag, which is used to house CSS style rules for an entire HTML document, is not well supported, sometimes stripped entirely, causing in-line style declarations to be the de facto standard, even though they are not optimal from a semantic web point of view. Many HTML-based GUI email clients automatically convert common plain text characters, like—and ", into their proper typographic equivalents, like—and ", which are not part of 7-bit ASCII. This can cause translation problems in other users' clients. Unicode supports many such complex characters, but font support issues with Unicode limit the usefulness of this possibility.

Style

Some senders may excessively rely upon large, colourful, or distracting fonts, making messages more difficult to read. Those who especially dislike certain types of formatting can override them in their user agent while still seeing other formatting and getting the other benefits of HTML. For instance, Mozilla Thunderbird makes it easy to specify a minimum font size.

Multi-part Formats

Many e-mail clients are configured to automatically generate a plain text version of a message and send it along with the HTML version, to ensure that it can be read even by text-only e-mail clients, using the Content-Type: multipart/alternative, as specified in RFC 1521. The message itself is of type multipart/alternative, and contains two parts, the first of type text/plain, which is read by text-only clients, and the second with text/html, which is read by HTML-capable clients. The plain text version may be missing important formatting information, however. Many mailing lists deliberately block HTML e-mail, either stripping out the HTML part to just leave the plain text part or rejecting the entire message.

Message Size

HTML e-mail is larger than plain text. Even if no special formatting is used, there will be the overhead from the tags used in a minimal HTML document, and if formatting is heavily used it may be much higher. Multi-part messages, with duplicate copies of the same content in different formats, increase the size even further.

Although the difference in download time between plain text and mixed message mail (which can be a factor of ten or more) was of concern in the 1990s , on a modern connection the difference is negligible, especially when compared to images, music files, or other common attachments.

Security Vulnerabilities

HTML allows for a link to have a different target than the link's text. This can be used in phishing attacks, in which users are fooled into believing that a link points to the website of an authoritative source (such as a bank), visiting it, and unintentionally revealing personal details (like bank account numbers) to a scammer.

If an e-mail contains web bugs (inline content from an external server, such as a picture), the server can alert a third party that the e-mail has been opened. This is a potential privacy risk, revealing that an e-mail address is real (so that it can be targeted in the future) and revealing when the message was read. For this reason, some e-mail clients do not load external images until requested to by the user.

During periods of increased network threats, the US Department of Defence converts all incoming html e-mail to text e-mail. The multipart type is intended to show the same content in different ways, but this is sometimes abused; some e-mail spam takes advantage of the format to trick spam filters into believing that the message is legitimate. They do this by including innocuous content in the text part of the message and putting the spam in the HTML part (which is what displays to the user). Most e-mail spam is sent in HTML for these reasons, so spam filters sometimes give higher spam scores to HTML messages.

Enriched Text

Enriched text is a formatted text format for e-mail, defined by the IETF in RFC 1896 and associated with the text/enriched MIME type. It is "intended to facilitate the wider interoperation of simple enriched text across a wide variety of hardware and software platforms". Today, enriched text is almost unknown in e-mail traffic, while HTML mail is widely used. Some people see enriched text, or at least the subset of HTML that can be transformed into enriched text, as a superior format for use with e-mail (mainly because of security considerations).

It should not be confused with Rich Text Format which is an entirely different specification, devised by Microsoft. A predecessor of this MIME type was called "text/richtext" in RFC 1341 and 1521. A single newline in enriched text is treated as a space. Formatting commands are in the same style as SGML and HTML. They must be balanced and nested. These are in other words two examples of valid enriched text:

<bold><italic>Hello, world!</italic></bold>

<italic><bold>Hello, world!</bold></italic>

The following, on the other hand, is not:

<bold><italic>Hello, world!</bold></italic>

Example:

As an example, the following enriched text:

<color><param>red</param>Blood</color> is <bold>thicker</bold> than

<color><param>blue</param>water</color>.

<paraindent><param>left</param><italic>— Well-known proverb

</italic></paraindent>

MHTML

MHTML stands for MIME HTML (Multipurpose Internet Mail Extension HTML). It is a proposed standard (in 1999 and not yet approved) for including resources that in usual HTTP pages are linked externally, such as images and sound files, in the same file as the HTML code, based on RFC 2557. The included data files are encoded using MIME. This format is sometimes referred to as MHT, after the suffix .mht given to such files by default when created by Microsoft Word, Internet Explorer or Opera.

The key to MHTML is that the content is encoded as if it were an HTML email message, using the MIME type multipart/related. The first part is the HTML file, encoded normally. Subsequent parts are additional resources, identified by their original URLs.

Web Browser Support

The process for saving a web page along with its resources as an MHTML file is not entirely standardised across browsers that support it. Due to this, the same web page saved as an MHTML file using different browsers may render somewhat differently on each browser.

Internet explorer

The .mht format was introduced in 1999 with Internet Explorer 5, which allows users to save a web page and its resources as a single MHTML file; a "Web Archive". This feature, however, may be unable to save certain complex web pages correctly, especially those containing scripts. All images etc will be saved as a single entity.

Opera

Support for saving a web page including its resources as an MHTML file was made available in the Opera 9.0 web browser since the weekly build 8265 (released on March 10, 2006).

Firefox

The web browser Mozilla Firefox, as of version 2, does not include direct support for saving or opening web pages as MHTML files (which is filed as bug 18764). This functionality can be obtained on Windows and Linux operating systems by installing a freely available third-party XPI file from Mozilla Archive Format extension, though the .mht files it generates are not fully compatible with Microsoft's products. As of August 2006, the available version of the MAF extension (V.0.6.3) cannot be installed into versions of Firefox greater than 1.5. A repackaged version is available on The Extensions Mirror.

Safari

As of version 2.0 (released April 29, 2005), Apple Computer's Safari web browser neither reads nor writes MHTML files. It does include a feature for saving web pages as archives which are seen as single files in Mac OS X's Finder, but they are actually directories containing the HTML page and its linked files.

Konqueror

As of version 3.5.7 (released 2007-05-02), KDE's Konqueror web browser does not support MHTML files. However, it does include a feature for saving web pages as single files which are actually gzipped tars.

4

E-mail Art

E-mail art (sometimes called "Electronic Mail Art") is simply any kind of art sent by e-mail. It includes computer graphics, animations, screensavers, digital scans of artwork in other media, or even ASCII art. When exhibited, e-mail art can be either displayed on a computer screen or similar type of display device, or the art can be printed out and displayed.

There is an ongoing debate among some artists as to just what the relationship of e-mail art to mail art should be considered to be. In addition to questions about whether this is even a valid or meaningful genre of art, as clearly almost any kind of digital-based art can be e-mailed, thus making it into "e-mail art," has been particular criticism of e-mail art by tradition-minded mail artists when the e-mail art has been perceived to be akin to mass media.

Other criticisms of e-mail art from a mail artist's perspective have focused on the lack of dimensionality of the attachment, the lack of intimacy as opposed to real mail. Many of the criticisms overlap those levelled against the Internet and World Wide Web in general.

Computer Graphics

Computer graphics is a sub-field of computer science and is concerned with digitally synthesizing and manipulating visual content. Although the term often refers to three-dimensional computer graphics, it also encompasses two-dimensional graphics and image processing. Computer graphics is often differentiated from the field of visualisation, although the two have many similarities.

A broad classification of major subfields in computer graphics might be:

— Geometry: studies ways to represent and process surfaces

— Animation: studies with ways to represent and manipulate motion

— Rendering: studies algorithms to reproduce light transport

— Imaging: studies image acquisition or image editing

Geometry Computer Graphics

The subfield of geometry studies the representation of three-dimensional objects in a discrete digital setting. Because the appearance of an object depends largely on the exterior of the object, boundary representations are most common in computer graphics. Two dimensional surfaces are a good analogy for the objects most often used in graphics, though quite often these objects are non-manifold.

Since surfaces are not finite, a discrete digital approximation is required: polygonal meshes (and to a lesser extent subdivision surfaces) are by far the most common representation, although point-based representations have been gaining some popularity in recent years. These representations are Lagrangian, meaning the spatial locations of the samples are independent.

In recent years, however, Eulerian surface descriptions (i.e., where spatial samples are fixed) such as level sets have been developed into a useful representation for deforming surfaces which undergo many topological changes.

Subfield of geometry

— Constructive solid geometry - Process by which complicated objects are modelled with implicit geometric objects and boolean operations

— Discrete differential geometry - a nascent field which defines geometric quantities for the discrete surfaces used in computer graphics.

— Digital geometry processing - surface reconstruction, simplification, fairing, mesh repair, parameterisation, remeshing, mesh generation, surface compression, and surface editing all fall under this heading.

— Point-based graphics - a recent field which focuses on points as the fundamental representation of surfaces.

— Simulation

— Subdivision surfaces

Subfield of Animation

The subfield of animation studies descriptions for surfaces (and other phenomena) that move or deform over time. Historically most interest in this area has been focused on parametric and data-driven models, but in recent years physical simulation has experienced a renaissance due to the growing computational capacity of modern machines.

Rendering

Rendering converts a model into an image either by simulating light transport to get physically-based photorealistic images, or by applying some kind of style as in non-photorealistic rendering. The two basic operations in realistic rendering are transport (how much light gets from one place to another) and scattering (how surfaces interact with light).

Transport

Transport describes how illumination in a scene gets from one place to another. Visibility is a major component of light transport.

Scattering and shading

Models of scattering and shading are used to describe the appearance of a surface. Although these issues may seem like a problems all on their own, they are studied almost exclusively within the context of rendering. Shading can be broken down into two orthogonal issues, which are often studied independently:

— scattering - how light interacts with the surface at a given point

— shading - how material properties vary across the surface

The former problem refers to scattering, i.e., the relationship between incoming and outgoing illumination at a given point. Descriptions of scattering are usually given in terms of a bidirectional scattering distribution function or BSDF. The latter issue addresses how different types of scattering are distributed across the surface (i.e., which scattering function applies where). Descriptions of this kind are typically expressed with a programme called a shader.

Other subfields

- physically-based rendering - concerned with generating images according to the laws of geometric optics
- real time rendering - focuses on rendering for interactive applications, typically using specialised hardware like GPUs
- non-photorealistic rendering
- relighting - recent area concerned with quickly re-rendering scenes

History of Computer Animation

One of the first displays of computer animation was Futureworld (1976), which included an animation of a human face and hand - produced by Ed Catmull and Fred Parke at the University of Utah.

There are several international conferences and journals where the most significant results in computer graphics are published. Among them are the SIGGRAPH and Eurographics conferences and the Association for Computing Machinery (ACM) Transactions on Graphics journal. The joint Eurographics and ACM SIGGRAPH symposium series features the major venues for the more specialised sub-fields: Symposium on Geometry Processing,Symposium on Rendering, and Symposium on Computer Animation.

Computer Animation

Computer animation is the art of creating moving images via the use of computers. It is a subfield of computer graphics and animation. Increasingly it is created by means of 3D computer graphics, though 2D computer graphics are still widely used for low bandwidth and faster real-time rendering needs. Sometimes the target of the animation is the computer itself, but it sometimes the target is another medium, such as film. It is also referred to as CGI (Computer-generated imagery or computer-generated imaging), especially when used in films.

To create the illusion of movement, an image is displayed on the computer screen then quickly replaced by a new image that is similar to the previous image, but shifted slightly. This technique is identical to how the illusion of movement is achieved with television and motion pictures.

Computer animation is essentially a digital successor to the art of stop motion animation of 3D models and frame-by-frame animation of 2D illustrations. For 3D animations, objects (models) are built on the computer monitor (modeled) and 3D figures are rigged with a virtual skeleton. For 2D figure animations, separate objects (illustrations) and separate transparent layers are used, with or without a virtual skeleton. Then the limbs, eyes, mouth, clothes, etc. of the figure are moved by the animator on key frames. The differences in appearance between key frames are automatically calculated by the computer in a process known as tweening or morphing. Finally, the animation is rendered.

For 3D animations, all frames must be rendered after modeling is complete. For 2D vector animations, the rendering process is the key frame illustration process, while tweened frames are rendered as needed. For prerecorded presentations, the rendered frames are transferred to a different format or medium such as film or digital video. The frames may also be rendered in real time as they are presented to the end-user audience. Low bandwidth animations transmitted via the internet (e.g. 2D Flash, X3D) often use software on the end-users computer to render in real time as an alternative to streaming or pre-loaded high bandwidth animations.

Creating Characters

Computer animation combines vector graphics with programmed movement. The starting point is often a stick figure in which the position of each feature (limb, mouth etc) is defined by as Avars (animation variable).

The character "Woody" in Toy Story, for example, uses 700 Avars, with 100 Avars in his face alone. Successive sets of Avars control all movement of the character from frame to frame. Once the stick model is moving in the desired way, the avars are incorporated into a full wire frame model or a model built of polygons. Finally surfaces are added, requiring a lengthy process of rendering to produce the final scene.

There are several ways of generating the Avar values to obtain realistic motion. Motion tracking uses lights or markers on a real person acting out the part, tracked by a video camera. Or the Avars may be set manually using a joystick or other form of input control. Toy Story uses no motion tracking, probably because only manual control by a skilled animator can produce effects not easily acted out by a real person.

Computer animation development equipment

Computer animation can be created with a computer and animation software. Some examples of animation software are: Amorphium, Art of Illusion, Poser, Ray Dream Studio, Bryce, Maya, Blender, TrueSpace, Lightwave, 3D Studio Max, SoftImage XSI, Alice, and Adobe Flash (2D). There are many more. Prices will vary greatly depending on target market. Some impressive animation can be achieved even with basic programmes; however, the rendering can take a lot of time on an ordinary home computer. Because of this, video game animators tend to use low resolution, low polygon count renders, such that the graphics can be rendered in real time on a home computer. Photorealistic animation would be impractical in this context.

Professional animators of movies, television, and video sequences on computer games make photorealistic animation with high detail. This level of quality for movie animation would take tens to hundreds of years to create on a home computer. Many powerful workstation computers are used instead. Graphics workstation computers use two to four processors, and thus are a lot more powerful than a home computer, and are specialised for rendering. A large number of workstations (known as a render farm) are networked together to effectively act as a giant computer. The result is a computer animated movie that can be completed in about one to five years (this process is not comprised solely of rendering, however).

A workstation typically costs $2,000 to $16,000, with the more expensive stations being able to render much faster, due to the more technologically advanced hardware that they contain. Pixar's Renderman is rendering software which is widely used as the movie animation industry standard, in competition with Mental Ray. It can be bought at the official Pixar website for about $5,000 to $8,000. It will work on Linux, Mac OS X, and Microsoft Windows based graphics workstations along with an animation programme such as Maya and Softimage XSI. Professionals also use digital movie cameras, motion capture or performance capture, bluescreens, film editing software, props, and other tools for movie animation.

Hardware Animation

The computer can draw the image, making any necessary changes to it before it is done. While the computer is rendering, the screen is showing the contents of what is called the primary or active buffer.

When the image is completed, the computer tells the screen to draw from the back buffer. This can be done in one of two ways: the contents of the back buffer can be copied to the primary buffer (or active buffer-the buffer which is currently being shown) or the computer can switch where it is drawing from and make the back buffer the new primary buffer. In this case, the primary buffer becomes the back buffer. John MacArthur is the one that thought up this process. This process is usually called double buffering or, informally, "flipping," because the computer is flipping its use of primary and back buffers.

This switching should be carried out when it is imperceptible to the user. Therefore it needs to take place during what is called the "v-sync" or vertical retrace. The v-sync, in CRTs, takes place when the electron guns reach the bottom right of the screen and need to reposition the beam to the top left of the screen. This happens very quickly and the image the guns had just projected remain on the screen as they are moving back to their starting position. While the guns are repositioning themselves, the computer has enough time to flip buffers and the new image will be rendered on the screen on the next pass of the guns. The new image will continued to be displayed until the buffers are flipped once more.

When the computer fails to wait for the v-sync, a condition called sprite breakup or image breakup is perceptible. This is highly undesirable and should always be avoided when possible to maintain the illusion of movement.

One open challenge in computer animation is a photorealistic animation of humans. Currently, most computer-animated movies show animal characters

(Finding Nemo), fantasy characters (Shrek, Monsters Inc.), anthropomorphic machines (Cars, Robots) or cartoon-like humans (The Incredibles). The movie Final Fantasy: The Spirits Within is often cited as the first computer-generated movie to attempt to show realistic-looking humans. However, due to the enormous complexity of the human body, human motion, and human biomechanics, realistic simulation of humans remains largely an open problem. It is one of the "holy grails" of computer animation.

Eventually, the goal is to create software where the animator can generate a movie sequence showing a photorealistic human character, undergoing physically-plausible motion, together with clothes, photorealistic hair, a complicated natural background, and possibly interacting with other simulated human characters. This could be done in a way that the viewer is no longer able to tell if a particular movie sequence is computer-generated, or created using real actors in front of movie cameras. Complete human realism is not likely to happen very soon, however such concepts obviously bear certain philosophical implications for the future of the film industry.

For the moment it looks like three dimensional computer animation can be divided into two main directions; photorealistic and non-photorealistic rendering. Photorealistic computer animation can itself be divided into two subcategories; real photorealism (where performance capture is used in the creation of the virtual human characters) and stylised photorealism. Real photorealism is what Final Fantasy tried to achieve and will in the future most likely have the ability to give us live action fantasy features as The Dark Crystal without having to use advanced puppetry and animatronics, while Antz is an example on stylistic photorealism (in the future stylized photorealism will be able to replace traditional stop motion animation as in Corpse Bride). None of them are as mentioned perfected yet, but the progress continues.

The non-photorealistic/cartoonish direction is more like an extension of traditional animation, an attempt to make the animation look like a three dimensional version of a cartoon, still using and perfecting the main principles of animation articulated by the Nine Old Men, such as squash and stretch.

While a single frame from a photorealistic computer animated feature will look like a photo if done right, a single frame vector from a cartoonish computer animated feature will look like a painting.

In 2D computer animation, moving objects are often referred to as "sprites." A sprite is an image that has a location associated with it. The location of the sprite is changed slightly, between each displayed frame, to make the sprite appear to move. The following pseudocode makes a sprite move from left to right:

```
var int x := 0, y := screenHeight &div; 2; while x < screenWidth

drawBackground()

drawSpriteAtXY (x, y) // draw on top of the background

x := x + 5 // move to the right
```

Modern (2001) computer animation uses different techniques to produce animations. Most frequently, sophisticated mathematics is used to manipulate complex three dimensional polygons, apply "textures", lighting and other effects to the polygons and finally rendering the complete image. A sophisticated graphical user interface may be used to create the animation and arrange its choreography. Another technique called constructive solid geometry defines objects by conducting boolean operations on regular shapes, and has the advantage that animations may be accurately produced at any resolution.

Let's step through the rendering of a simple image of a room with flat wood walls with a grey pyramid in the center of the room. The pyramid will have a spotlight shining on it. Each wall, the floor and the ceiling is a simple polygon, in this case, a rectangle. Each corner of the rectangles is defined by three values referred to as X, Y and Z. X is how far left and right the point is. Y is how far up and down the point is, and Z is far in and out of the screen the point is. The wall nearest us would be defined by four points: (in the order x, y, z). Below is a representation of how the wall is defined.

(0, 10, 0) (10, 10, 0)

(0,0,0) (10, 0, 0)

The far wall would be:

(0, 10, 20) (10, 10, 20)

(0, 0, 20) (10, 0, 20)

The pyramid is made up of five polygons: the rectangular base, and four triangular sides. To draw this image the computer uses math to calculate how to project this image, defined by three dimensional data, onto a two dimensional computer screen.

First where our view point is, that is, from what vantage point will the scene be drawn. Our view point is inside the room a bit above the floor, directly in front of the pyramid. First the computer will calculate which polygons are visible. The near wall will not be displayed at all, as it is behind our view point. The far side of the pyramid will also not be drawn as it is hidden by the front of the pyramid.

Next each point is perspective projected onto the screen. The portions of the walls 'farthest' from the view point will appear to be shorter than the nearer areas due to perspective. To make the walls look like wood, a wood pattern, called a texture, will be drawn on them. To accomplish this, a technique called "texture mapping" is often used. A small drawing of wood that can be repeatedly drawn in a matching tiled pattern (like wallpaper) is stretched and drawn onto the walls' final shape. The pyramid is solid grey so sp its surfaces can just be rendered as grey. But we also have a spotlight. Where its light falls we lighten colors, where objects blocks the light we darken colors.

Movies

CGI short films have been produced as independent animation since the 1976, though the popularity of computer animation (especially in the field of special effects) skyrocketed during the modern era of U.S. animation. The first completely computer-generated animated movie was Toy Story.

Amateur Animation

The popularity of sites such as YouTube, which allows members to upload their own movies for others to view, has created a growing number of what is often considered amateur computer animators. With many free utilities available and programmes such as Windows Movie Maker, anyone with the tools can have their animation viewed by thousands.

Architectural Animation

Architects use services from animation companies to create

a 3-dimensional models for both the customers and builders. It can be more accurate than traditional drawings. Architectural animation can also be used to see the possible relationship the building will have in relation to the environment and its surrounding buildings.

Computer-generated imagery (CGI)

Computer-generated imagery (commonly abbreviated as CGI) is the application of the field of computer graphics (or more specifically, 3D computer graphics) to special effects in films, television programmes, commercials, simulators and simulation generally, and printed media. Video games usually use real-time computer graphics (rarely referred to as CGI), but may also include pre-rendered "cut scenes" and intro movies that would be typical CGI applications. These are referred to as FMV.

CGI is used for visual effects because effects are more controllable than other more physically based processes, such as constructing miniatures for effects shots or hiring extras for crowd scenes, and because it allows the creation of images that would not be feasible using any other technology. It can also allow a single artist to produce content without the use of actors, expensive set pieces, or props.

Computer software such as Maya and Softimage XSI are used to make computer-generated imagery for movies, etc. Recent accessibility of CGI software and increased computer speeds has allowed individual artists and small companies to produce professional grade films, games, and fine art from their home computers. This has brought about an Internet subculture with its own set of global celebrities, clichés, and technical vocabulary.

Simulators, particularly flight simulators, and

simulation generally, make extensive use of CGI techniques for representing the Outside World (OTW).

Companies making the highest levels of flight simulators such as the so-called 'Level D' (the highest technical level for civil aircraft training and recognised on both sides of the Atlantic) normally produce their own CGI system for use in their simulators. Other simulator companies buy in a CGI system from a specialist supplier. Companies making Level D flight simulators include CAE (Canada, Germany and USA), FSI (USA), Link division of L-3 Communications, Lockheed Martin (Orlando), Rockwell Collins (USA) and Thales (France and UK)

2D CGI was first used in movies in 1973's Westworld, though the first use of 3D imagery was in its sequel, Futureworld (1976), which featured a computer-generated hand and face created by then University of Utah graduate students Edwin Catmull and Fred Parke. The third movie to use this technology was Star Wars (1977) for the scenes with the Death Star plans. The first two films to make heavy investments in CGI, Tron (1982) and The Last Starfighter (1984), were commercial failures, causing most directors to relegate CGI to images that were supposed to look like they were created by a computer.

The first real CGI character was created by Pixar for the film Young Sherlock Holmes in 1985 (not counting the simple polyhedron character Bit in Tron). It took the form of a knight composed of elements from a stained glass window. CGI did not win over the motion picture industry until 1989, however, when The Abyss won the Academy Award for Visual Effects. Industrial Light and Magic (ILM) produced complex CGI visual effects, most notably a seawater creature dubbed the pseudopod, featuring in one scene of the film. CGI then took a central role in Terminator 2: Judgment Day (1991), in which the T-1000

Terminator villain wowed audiences with liquid metal and morphing effects fully integrated into action sequences throughout the film. Terminator 2 also won ILM an Oscar for its effects.

It was the 1993 film Jurassic Park, however, in which dinosaurs created with CGI were seamlessly integrated into live action scenes, that revolutionised the movie industry. It marked Hollywood's transition from stop-motion animation and conventional optical effects to digital techniques.

The following year, CGI was used to create the special effects for Forrest Gump. The most noteworthy effects shots were the digital removal of actor Gary Sinise's legs. Other effects included a napalm strike, the fast-moving Ping-Pong balls, and the digital insertion of Tom Hanks into several scenes of historical footage.

2D CGI increasingly appeared in traditionally animated films, where it supplemented the use of hand-illustrated cels. Its uses ranged from digital tweening motion between frames, to eye-catching quasi-3D effects such as the ballroom scene in Beauty and the Beast.

In 1994, the hit Canadian show ReBoot was aired and was credited with being the first full length, completely computer animated TV series.

In 1995, the first fully computer-generated feature film, Pixar's (The Walt Disney Company) Toy Story, was a resounding commercial success. Additional digital animation studios such as Blue Sky Studios (Fox), DNA Productions (Paramount Pictures and Warner Bros.), Omation Studios (Paramount Pictures), Sony Pictures Animation (Columbia Pictures), Vanguard Animation (Walt Disney Pictures, Lions Gate Films and 20th Century Fox), Big Idea Productions (Universal Pictures and FHE

Pictures),Animal Logic (Warner Bros) and Pacific Data Images (Dreamworks SKG) went into production, and existing animation companies such as The Walt Disney Company began to make a transition from traditional animation to CGI.

Between 1995 and 2005 the average effects budget for a wide-release feature film skyrocketed from $5 million to $40 million. According to one studio executive, as of 2005, more than half of feature films have significant effects. Although, CGI has made up for the expenditures by grossing over 20% more than their real-life counterparts.

In the early 2000s, computer-generated imagery became the dominant form of special effects. The technology progressed to the point that it became possible to include virtual stunt doubles. Camera tracking software was refined to allow increasingly complex visual effects developments that were previously impossible. Computer-generated extras also became used extensively in crowd scenes with advanced flocking and crowd simulation software. The timeline of CGI in movies shows a detailed list of pioneering uses of computer-generated imagery in film and television.

CGI for films is usually rendered at about 1.4-6 megapixels. Toy Story, for example, was rendered at 1536 × 922 (1.42MP). The time to render one frame is typically around 2-3 hours, with ten times that for the most complex scenes. This time hasn't changed much in the last decade, as image quality has progressed at the same rate as improvements in hardware, since with faster machines, more and more complexity becomes feasible. Exponential increases in GPUs processing power, as well as massive increases in parallel CPU power, storage and memory speed and size have greatly increased CGI's potential.

In 2001, Square Pictures created the CGI film Final Fantasy: The Spirits Within, which made headlines for attempting to create photo-realistic human actors. The film was not a box-office success. Some commentators have suggested this may be partly because the lead CGI characters had facial features which fell into the uncanny valley. After creating one more film using a similar visual style (Final Flight of the Osiris, a short film which served as a prologue to The Matrix Reloaded), Square Pictures closed down.

Another production which uses CGI almost entirely is Code Lyoko, a youth television show regarding a virtual world called Lyoko, it's gateway to the real world, and the computer programme planning to take over the world, Xana (Code Lyoko). The show is partially 2D animated, and partially CGI animated. 2D animation describes the real world, where CGI rendering describes the virtual world of Lyoko, after the show's main characters have been scanned and converted into it.

Developments in CGI technologies are reported each year at SIGGRAPH, an annual conference on computer graphics and interactive techniques, attended each year by tens of thousands of computer professionals. Developers of computer games and 3D video cards strive to achieve the same visual quality on personal computers in real-time as is possible for CGI films and animation. With the rapid advancement of real-time rendering quality, artists began to use game engines to render non-interactive movies. This art form is called machinima.

Creating Characters

3D computer animation combines 3D modeling with programmed movement. Models are constructed out of geometrical vertices, faces, and edges in a true 3D coordinate system. Objects are sculpted much like real clay or plaster, working from general forms to specific details with various sculpting tools. A bone/joint system is set up to deform the 3d mesh ie. to make a humanoid model walk. In a process called rigging, the virtual marionette is given various controllers and handles for an animator to manipulate.

The character "Woody" in Pixar's movie Toy Story, for example, uses 700 specialised animation controllers. Rhythm and Hues Studios labored for two years to create Aslan in the movie Chronicles of Narnia which had about 1851 controllers, 742 in just the face alone. In the 2004 film The Day After Tomorrow, designers had to design forces of extreme weather with the help of video references and accurate meteorological facts.

For the 2005 remake of King Kong, actor Andy Serkis was used to help designers pinpoint the gorilla's prime location in the shots and used his expressions to model "human" characteristics onto the creature. Toho Studios has famously (or infamously) refused to portray the popular Godzilla character using CGI, with the reason being that they have always used suitmation and CGI would somehow take the "life" out of the character.

Digital Grading

One of the less obvious CGI effects in movies is digital grading. This is a computer process in which sections of the original image are color-corrected using special processing software. A detail that was too dark in the original shot can be lit and enhanced in this post-production process. For example, in Star Trek: First Contact, digital grading was used to turn Picard's face blue as his Borg assimilation is shown, and in The Lord of the Rings, digital grading was used to drain the color from

Boromir's face as he died.

Motion Capture

Motion capture, motion tracking, or mocap is a technique of digitally recording movements for entertainment, sports and medical applications.

Methods and Systems of Motion Capture

Motion tracking or motion capture started as a photogrametric analysis tool in biomechanics research in the 1970s and 1980s, and expanded into education, training, sports and recently computer animation for cinema and video games as the technology matured. A performer wears markers near each joint to identify the motion by the positions or angles between the markers. Acoustic, inertial, LED, magnetic or reflective markers, or combinations of any of these, are tracked, optimally at least two times the rate of the desired motion, to submillimeter positions. The motion capture computer software records the positions, angles, velocities, accelerations and impulses, providing an accurate digital representation of the motion.

In entertainment applications this can reduce the costs of animation which otherwise requires the animator to draw each frame, or with more sophisticated software, key frames which are interpolated by the software. Motion capture saves time and creates more natural movements than manual animation, but is limited to motions that are anatomically possible. Some applications might require additional impossible movements like animated super hero martial arts or stretching and squishing that are not possible with real actors.

In biomechanics, sports and training, real time data can provide the necessary information to diagnose problems or suggest ways to improve performance, requiring motion capture technology to capture motions up to 140 miles per hour for a golf swing.

Optical Systems

Optical systems triangulate the 3D position of a marker between one or more cameras calibrated to provide overlapping projections. Tracking a large number of markers or multiple performers or expanding the capture area is accomplished by the addition of more cameras. These systems produce data with 3 degrees of freedom for each marker, and rotational information must be inferred from the relative orientation of three or more markers; for instance shoulder, elbow and wrist markers providing the angle of the elbow...

Passive optical system

Passive optical system use markers coated with a Retroreflective material to reflect light back that is generated near the cameras lens. The cameras sensitivity can be adjusted taking advantage of most cameras narrow range of sensitivity to light so only the bright markers will be sampled ignoring skin and fabric.

The centroid of the marker is estimated as a position within the 2 dimensional image that is captured. The grayscale value of each pixel can be used to provide sub-pixel accuracy. An object with markers attached at known positions is used to calibrate the cameras and obtain their positions and the lens distortion of each camera is measured. Providing two calibrated cameras see a marker, a 3 dimensional fix can be obtained. Typically a system will consist of around 6 to 24 cameras. Systems of over two hundred cameras exist. Extra cameras are required for full coverage around the capture subject. Typical eight camera systems are about $150,000 US.

Professional vendors have sophisticated constraint software to reduce problems from marker swapping since all markers appear identical. Unlike active marker systems and magnetic systems, passive systems do not require the user to wear wires or electronic equipment. The markers are usually attached directly to the skin (as in biomechanics), or they are velcroed to a performer wearing a full body spandex/lycra suit designed specifically for motion capture. This type of system can capture large numbers of markers at frame rates as high as 2000fps with high accuracy. The frame rate for a given system is often traded off between resolution and speed so a 4 megapixel system runs at 160 hertz normally but can reduce the resolution to 1 megapixel and then run a 640 hertz for a constant 640 million pixels per second.

Active optical system

Active optical systems triangulate positions by illuminating one LED at a time very quickly or multiple LEDs but sophisticated software to identify them by their relative positions, somewhat akin to celestial navigation. Rather than reflecting light back that is generated externally, the markers themselves are powered to emit their own light. Since Inverse Square law provides 1/4 the power at 2 times the distance, this can increase the distances and volume for capture. ILM used active Markers in Van Helsing to allow capture of the Harpies on very large sets. The power to each marker can be provided sequentially in phase with the capture system providing a unique identification of each marker for a given capture frame at a cost to the resultant frame rate. The ability to identify each marker in this manner is useful in realtime applications. The alternative method of identifying markers is to do it algorithmically requiring extra processing of the data.

Time modulated optical system

Active marker systems can further be refined by strobing one marker on at a time, or tracking multiple markers over time and modulating the amplitude or pulse width to provide marker ID. 12 megapixel spatial resolution modulated systems show more subtle movements than 4 megapixel optical systems by having both higher spatial and temporal resolution. Directors can see the actors performance in real time, and watch the results on the mocap driven CG character. The unique marker IDs reduce the turnaround, by eliminating marker swapping and providing much cleaner data than other technologies. LEDs with onboard processing and a radio synchronization allow motion capture outdoors in direct sunlight, while capturing at 480 frames per second due to a high speed electronic shutter.

Computer processing of modulated IDs allows less hand cleanup or filtered results for lower operational costs. This higher accuracy and resolution requires more processing than passive technologies, but the additional processing is done at the camera to improve resolution via a subpixel or centroid processing, providing both high resolution and high speed. These motion capture systems are typically under $50,000 for an eight camera, 12 megapixel spatial resolution 480 hertz system with one actor.

Semi-passive Imperceptible Marker

One can reverse the traditional approach based on high speed cameras. Systems such as Prakash use inexpensive high speed projectors. The specially built IR projectors optically encode the space. Instead of retro-reflective or active light emitting diode (LED) markers, the system uses photosensitive marker tags to decode the optical signals. By attaching tags with photosensors to scene points, the tags can compute not only their own locations of each point, but also their own orientation, incident illumination, and reflectance.

These tracking tags that work in natural lighting conditions and can be imperceptibly embedded in attire or other objects. The system supports an unlimited number of tags in a scene, with each tag uniquely identified to eliminate marker reacquisition issues. Since the system eliminates a high speed camera and the corresponding high-speed image stream, it requires significantly lower data bandwidth. The tags also provide incident illumination data which can be used to match scene lighting when inserting synthetic elements. The technique is therefore ideal for on-set motion capture or real-time broadcasting of virtual sets.

Non-Optical Systems

Inertial Motion Capture technology is based on miniature inertial sensors, biomechanical models and sensor fusion algorithms. It's an easy to use and cost-efficient way for full-body human motion capture. The motion data of the inertial sensors (Inertial_guidance_system) is transmitted wirelessly to a PC or laptop, where the full body motion is recorded or viewed. No external cameras, emitters or markers are needed for relative motions.

Inertial mocap systems capture the full 6 degrees of freedom body motion of a human in real-time. Benefits of using Inertial systems include; No solving, freedom from studio's as most systems are portable, and large capture areas. These systems are similar to the WII controllers but much more sensitive and having much greater resolution and update rate. They can accurately measure the direction to the ground to within a degree. Base suits tend to be in the $50,000 range, however the cost of a system often relates to the quality of data it produces.

Mechanical motion capture systems

Mechanical motion capture systems directly track body joint angles and are often referred to as exo-skeleton motion capture systems, due to the way the sensors are attached to the body. A performer attaches the skeletal-like structure to their body and as they move so do the articulated mechanical parts, measuring the performer's relative motion. Mechanical motion capture systems are real-time, relatively low-cost, free-of-occlusion, and wireless (untethered) systems that have unlimited capture volume. Typically, they are rigid structures of jointed, straight metal or plastic rods linked together with potentiometers that articulate at the joints of the body. These suits tend to be in the $25,000 to $75,000 range plus an external absolution positioning system.

Magnetic systems

Magnetic systems calculate position and orientation by the relative magnetic flux of three orthogonal coils on both the transmitter and each receiver. The relative intensity of the voltage or current of the three coils allows these systems to calculate both range and orientation by meticulously mapping the tracking volume. Since the sensor output is 6DOF, useful results can be obtained with two-thirds the number of markers required in optical systems; one on upper arm and one on lower arm for elbow position and angle.

The markers are not occluded by nonmetallic objects

but are susceptible to magnetic and electrical interference from metal objects in the environment, like rebar (steel reinforcing bars in concrete) or wiring, which affect the magnetic field, and electrical sources such as monitors, lights, cables and computers. The sensor response is nonlinear, especially toward edges of the capture area. The wiring from the sensors tends to preclude extreme performance movements. The capture volumes for magnetic systems are dramatically smaller than they are for optical systems. With the magnetic systems, there is a distinction between "AC" and "DC" systems: one uses square pulses, the other uses sine wave pulse.

Procedure

In the motion capture session, the movements of one or more actors are sampled many times per second. High resolution optical motion capture systems can be used to sample body, facial and finger movement at the same time.

A motion capture session records only the movements of the actor, not his visual appearance. These movements are recorded as animation data which are mapped to a 3D model (human, giant robot, etc.) created by a computer artist, to move the model the same way. This is comparable to the older technique of rotoscope where the visual appearance of the motion of an actor was filmed, then the film used as a guide for the frame by frame motion of a hand-drawn animated character.

If desired, a camera can pan, tilt, or dolly around the stage while the actor is performing and the motion capture system can capture the camera and props as well. This allows the computer generated characters, images and sets, to have the same perspective as the video images from the camera. A computer processes the data and displays the movements of the actor, as inferred from the 3D position of each marker. If desired, a virtual or real camera can be tracked as well, providing the desired camera positions in terms of objects in the set.

A related technique match moving can derive 3D camera movement from a single 2D image sequence without the use of photogrammetry, but is often ambiguous below centimeter resolution, due to the inability to distinguish pose and scale characteristics from a single vantage point. One might extrapolate that future technology might include full-frame imaging from many camera angles to record the exact position of every part of the actor's body, clothing, and hair for the entire duration of the session, resulting in a higher resolution of detail than is possible today.

After processing, the software exports animation data, which computer animators can associate with a 3D model and then manipulate using normal computer animation software. If the actor's performance was good and the software processing was accurate, this manipulation is limited to placing the actor in the scene that the animator has created and controlling the 3D model's interaction with objects.

Motion capture began as a military technology used for tracking targets, using AC magnetic trackers. In 1986, marketer Jack Scully and engineer Ernie Blood were fired from Polhemus Navigation Services. They founded Ascension Technology, supplier of mocap devices. This began a revolution in motion capture for use in cartoons in the private sector. Chris Walker, an animator and inventor of animation technology, further developed motion capture, and used it in TV cartoons under his company Modern Cartoons in the 1990s. The mocap suit he used then cost $300,000 USD.

Advantages

Mo cap offers several advantages over traditional computer animation of a 3D model:

- More rapid, sometimes even real time results can be obtained.
- The amount of work does not vary with the complexity or length of the performance to the same degree when using traditional techniques.
- Complex movement and realistic physical interactions such as secondary animation, weight and exchange of forces can be more easily recreated in a physically accurate manner.
- Mocap technology allows one actor to play multiple roles within a single film.

Advantages over live action

In movies that contains CGI in such large amounts that the actors would have to stay in front of a bluescreen and interact with invisible computer animated characters which is added later, trying to fit into a computer animated world, it is sometimes less problematic to make everything digital, including the actors. This way, all elements would fit together naturally and have the same visual look.

- The director can choose any angle he or she desires from a scene, including angles that would have been hard or impossible in a live action movie.
- Limitless possibilities for rotating effect.
- Costumes, make-up, body size and age can be changed to whatever is needed.
- The characters will blend perfectly in with their digital environments.

— There is no need to have light, colors and filters in mind when filming the motions, as this will be added digitally later.

Disadvantages

— Specific hardware and special programmes are required to obtain and process the data.

— The cost of the software and equipment, personnel required can be prohibitive for small productions.

— The capture system may have specific requirements for the space it is operated in.

— When problems occur it is sometime easier to reshoot the scene rather than trying to manipulate the data. Only a few systems allow real time viewing of the data to decide if the take needs to be redone.

— Applying motion to quadruped characters can be difficult.

— The technology can become obsolete every few years as better software and techniques are invented.

— The results are limited to what can be performed within the capture volume without extra editing of the data.

— Movement that does not follow the laws of physics generally cannot be represented.

— Traditional animation techniques such as added emphasis on anticipation and follow through, secondary motion or manipulating the shape of the character as with squash and stretch animation techniques are generally not applicable.

— If the computer model has different proportions from the capture subject artifacts may occur. For example, if a cartoon character has large, over-sized hands, these may intersect strangely with any other body part when the human actor brings them too close to his body.

— The real life performance may not translate on to the computer model as expected.

Some video games use motion capture to animate athletes, martial artists, and other in-game characters. Movies use motion capture for CG effects, in some cases replacing traditional cell animation, and for completely computer-generated creatures, such as Gollum, The Mummy, and King Kong.

In producing entire feature films with Computer animation, the industry is currently split between studios that use Motion Capture, and studios that do not. Out of the three nominees for the 2006 Academy Award for Best Animated Feature, two of the nominees ("Monster House" and the winner "Happy Feet") used Motion Capture, and only Pixar's Cars was animated without Motion Capture. In the ending credits of Pixar's latest film "Ratatouille", a stamp appears labelling the film as "100% Pure Animation — No Motion Capture!" On the other hand, Pixar's parent The Walt Disney Company has announced that it will distribute Robert Zemeckis's A Christmas Carol to be produced using "Performance Capture," the motion-capture approach that Zemeckis first used on The Polar Express.

Virtual Reality and Augmented Reality allow users to interact with digital content in real-time. This can be useful for training simulations, visual perception tests, or performing a virtual walk-through in a 3D environment. Gait analysis is the major application of motion capture in clinical medicine. Motion capture technology is frequently used in digital puppetry systems to aid in the performance of computer generated characters in real-time.

Related Techniques of Motion Capture

Facial motion capture is utilised to record the complex movements in a human face, especially while speaking with emotion. This is generally performed with an optical setup using multiple cameras arranged in a hemisphere at close range, with small markers glued or taped to the actor's face.

Inertial systems use devices such as accelerometers or gyroscopes to measure positions and angles. They are often used in conjunction with other systems to provide updates and global reference, since they only measure relative changes, not absolute position.

RF (radio frequency) positioning systems are becoming more viable as higher frequency RF devices allow greater precision than older RF technologies. The speed of light is 30 centimeters per nanosecond (billionth of a second), so a 10 gigahertz (billion cycles per second) RF signal enables an accuracy of about 3 centimeters. By measuring amplitude to a quarter wavelength, it is possible to improve the resolution down to about 8 mm. To achieve the resolution of optical systems, frequencies of 50 gigahertz or higher are needed, which are almost as line of sight and as easy to block as optical systems. Multipath and reradiation of the signal are likely to cause additional problems, but these technologies will be ideal for tracking larger volumes with reasonable accuracy, since the required resolution at 100 meter distances isn't likely to be as high.

An alternative approach was developed where the actor is given an unlimited walking area through the use of a rotating sphere, similar to a hamster ball, which contains internal sensors recording the angular movements, removing the need for external cameras and other equipment. Even though this technology could potentially lead to much lower costs for mocap, the basic sphere is only capable of recording a single continuous direction. Additional sensors worn on the person would be needed to record anything more.

5

E-mail Authentication

Ensuring a valid identity on an e-mail has become a vital first step in stopping spam, forgery, fraud, and even more serious crimes. An essential second step would be ensuring the entity has a good reputation.

Unfortunately, the Simple Mail Transfer Protocol (SMTP) that handles most e-mail today was designed in the early 1980's when most Internet users were honest "techies" who expected others to be equally honest. This article will explain how e-mail identities are forged and the steps that are being taken now to prevent it..

Simple Mail transfer

In a simple mail transfer, there are four key players: the author or originator of the e-mail, the sender or agent who first puts the e-mail on the public Internet, the receiver or agent who receives the e-mail from the Internet, and the recipient who is the person intended to read the e-mail.

Other than the sender's IP address, there is no verification of any information in an e-mail. It is quite easy for a spammer to make an exact copy of an e-mail from smithbarney.com, including a long complicated sequence of headers and a genuine logo in the body of an e-mail, then change the content to send readers to a website that appears to be genuine, but is actually a phishing scam designed to capture names, passwords, and credit card numbers.

So why can't the sender's IP address be used to identify the spammer? There are two problems. One is that spammers often work through forwarders to hide their IP addresses. Another is that the sender is often a zombie that has been infected by a computer virus, and is programmed to send spam without the owner even knowing about it. There are millions of insecure home computers, and they have become a major source of spam.

Attempts to stop spam by blacklisting sender's IP addresses still allows a small percentage through. Most IP addresses are dynamic, i.e. they are frequently changing. An ISP, or any organisation directly connected to the Internet, gets a block of real Internet addresses when they register in the DNS. Within that block, they assign individual addresses to customers as needed. A dial-up customer may get a new IP address each time they connect. By the time that address appears on blacklists all over the world, the spammer will have new addresses for the next run. There are 4 billion possible IPv4 addresses on the Internet. The game of keeping up with these rapidly changing IP addresses has been facetiously called "whack-a-mole".

There are a number of things that ISPs have done to stop zombies and deliberate spamming by their customers. Infected computers can be cleared of viruses and patched to resist further infection. Outgoing e-mail can be monitored for any sudden increase in flow or in content that is typical of spam. Some ISPs have been quite successful, but others don't care to make the effort.

Role of Authenticating Senders

E-mail authentication greatly simplifies and automates the process of identifying senders. After identifying and verifying a claimed domain name, it is possible to treat suspected forgeries with suspicion, reject known forgeries, and block e-mail from known spamming domains. It is also possible to "whitelist" e-mail from known reputable domains, and bypass content-based filtering, which always loses some valid e-mails in the flood of spam. The fourth category, e-mail from unknown domains, can be treated like we now treat all e-mail—increasingly rigorous filtering, return challenges to the sender, etc. Success of a domain-rating system should encourage reputable ISPs to stop their outgoing spam and get a good rating.

There are a number of ways to authenticate a sender's domain name (SPF, CSV, SenderID, DomainKeys). All are very effective in stopping the kind of forgery now prevalent. None exclude the use of other methods, although SPF / CSV, SPF / SenderID, and SenderID / Domainkeys pairwise appear to be competing for the same niches. The most widely used will likely be the ones that require the least effort on the part of ISPs and others currently operating public mail servers.

SPF, CSV, and SenderID authenticate just a domain name. DomainKeys uses a digital signature to authenticate a domain name and the entire content of a message. SPF and CSV can reject a forgery before any data transfer. SenderID and DomainKeys must see at least the headers, so the entire message must be transmitted. SPF has a problem with forwarders, SenderID also with mailing lists. CSV is only about the HELO identity.

SPF, CSV, and SenderID work by tying a temporary IP address to a claimed domain name. Every incoming e-mail has an IP address that cannot be forged, a bunch of domain names in the e-mail headers, and a few more in the commands from the sender's SMTP server. The methods differ in which of these names to use as the sender's domain name. All of them can be faked, but what cannot be faked is a domain name held by a DNS server for that section of the Internet.

The simplest and by far most widely deployed authentication scheme begins with a reverse DNS lookup of the connecting IP address. If there is no answer, it's a safe bet that the address is not a legitimate sender. If there is an answer, a forward DNS lookup of that answer authenticates the sender if it returns the connecting IP address. In other words, we look up the name of the connecting IP address, and look up the IP address of that name, and they must match.

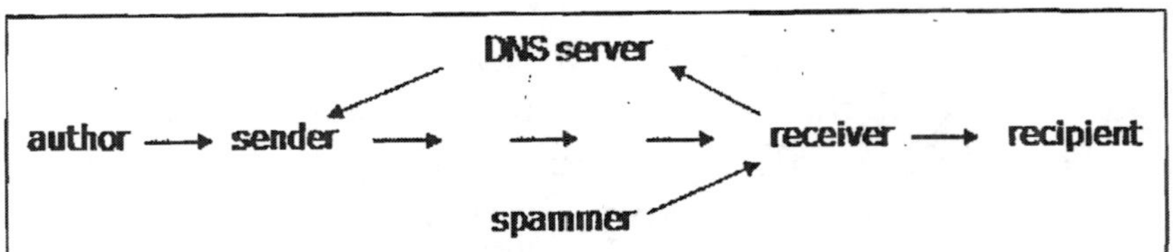

The procedure to authenticate is basically simple. When a request to deliver an e-mail arrives, the claimed sender's domain name is sent in a query to a high-level DNS server. That DNS server in turn, refers to lower level servers until an answer is found that is authoritative for the domain in question. The answer returned to the receiver includes the information to authenticate the e-mail. For SPF and SenderID, the query returns the IP addresses which are authorised to send mail on behalf of that domain. Typically there will be very few authorised SMTP sending addresses, even from a domain with millions of dynamically assignable IP addresses. For DomainKeys, the query returns the public key for the domain, which then validates the signature in an e-mail header.

A successful validation proves the email originated from the same people responsible for the DNS servers for that domain (as only the domain owners would have proper access to the private key that matches the public key published in DNS), and neither the headers nor the body of the e-mail were altered on its way from the sender.

A spammer has no access to any of the connections between these DNS servers. Even if he were to falsify records in the DNS server for his own domain, he would not be able to forge records for someone else's domain name. When a spammer tries to send an e-mail claiming to be from amazon.com, for example, the receiver queries the.com DNS server, then a server in a secure building at Amazon. The IP address on the message from the spammer won't match any of Amazon's authorised IP addresses, and the e-mail can be rejected. Alternatively, the DomainKey will show the signature in the e-mail is invalid because it is highly unlikely the spammer has access to the amazon.com private key.

Use of the DNS database to register authentication information for a domain is relatively new. The new information is added to existing DNS records, and queries for this information are handled the same way as any other DNS query. Publishing authentication records in DNS is voluntary, and many domains probably won't bother. However, any legitimate domain, even those that don't intend to operate public mail servers, will most likely want to block others from using their name to forge e-mails. A simple code in their DNS record will tell the world, "Block all mail claiming to be from our domain. We have no public mail servers."

E-MAIL FORWARDING

There are some additional details when an e-mail forwarder is involved. Forwarders perform a useful service in allowing you to have one simple permanent address, even if you change jobs or ISPs. List servers perform a similar function, forwarding e-mail to many receivers on behalf of one sender. Forwarders pose no problem for an end-to-end authentication method like DomainKeys, as long as the signed message is not modified.

CSV limits its focus to one-hop authentications. SPF and SenderID have in essence the same limitation, they don't work directly behind the "border" (MX) of the receiver. For SPF forwarders to third parties could rewrite the Return-Path (MAIL FROM) in a similar way like mailing lists.

For SenderID, forwarders to third parties and mailing lists are asked to add a Sender: or Resent-Sender: header. For many mailing lists, the former is already the case, but other forwarders avoid any modifications of the mail in addition to the mandatory Received-timestamp line.

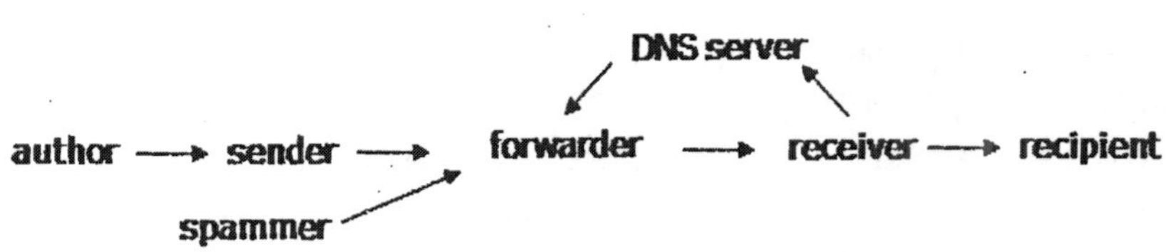

Use of a forwarder prevents the receiver from directly seeing the sender's IP address. The incoming IP packets have only the forwarder's IP address. Two solutions are possible if one can trust all forwarders. Either one trusts the forwarder to authenticate the sender, or one trusts the forwarder to at least accurately record the incoming IP address and pass it on, so one can do their own authentication.

The situation gets complicated when there is more than one forwarder. A sender can explicitly authorise a forwarder to send on its behalf, in effect extending its boundary to the public Internet. A receiver can trust a forwarder that it pays to handle e-mail, in effect designating a new receiver. There may be additional "MTA relays" in the middle, however. These are sometimes used for administrative control, traffic aggregation, and routing control. All it takes is one broken link in the chain-of-trust from sender to receiver, and it is no longer possible to authenticate the sender.

Forwarders have one other responsibility, and that is to route Delivery Status Notices (DSNs) and spam bounces properly. Normal DSNs should be sent straight to an address chosen by the sender. Spam bounces should not be sent to any address that may be forged. These bounces may go back by the same path they came, if that path has been authenticated.

Phishing Attempt

In computing, phishing is a criminal activity using social engineering techniques. Phishers attempt to fraudulently acquire sensitive information, such as usernames, passwords and credit card details, by masquerading as a trustworthy entity in an electronic communication. eBay and PayPal are two of the most targeted companies, and online banks are also common targets. Phishing is typically carried out by email or instant messaging, and often directs users to give details at a website, although phone contact has been used as well. Attempts to deal with the growing number of reported phishing incidents include legislation, user training, and technical measures.

The first recorded mention of the term phishing is on the alt.online-service. America-online Usenet newsgroup on January 2, 1996, although the term may have appeared even earlier in the print edition of the hacker magazine 2600. A phishing technique was described in detail as early as 1987, in a paper and presentation delivered to the International HP Users Group, Interex. The term phishing is a variant of fishing, probably influenced by phreaking, and alludes to the use of increasingly sophisticated lures to "fish" for a user's financial information and passwords. The word may also be linked to leetspeak, in which ph is a common substitution for f. The popular theory that it is a portmanteau of password harvesting is an example of folk etymology.

Current Status of Phishing

Early phishing

Those who would later phish on AOL during the 1990s originally used fake, algorithmically generated credit card numbers to create accounts on AOL, which could last weeks or even months. After AOL brought in measures in late 1995 to prevent this, early AOL crackers resorted to phishing for legitimate accounts.

Phishing on AOL was closely associated with the warez community that exchanged pirated software. A phisher might pose as an AOL staff member and send an instant message to a potential victim, asking him to reveal his password. In order to lure the victim into giving up sensitive information the message might include text such as "verify your account" or "confirm billing information". Once the victim had submitted his password, the attacker could access and use the victim's account for criminal purposes, such as spamming. Both phishing and warezing on AOL generally required custom-written programmes, such as AOHell. Phishing became so prevalent on AOL that they added a line on all instant messages stating: "no one working at AOL will ask for your password or billing information".

After 1997, AOL's policy enforcement with respect to phishing and warez became stricter and forced pirated software off AOL servers. AOL simultaneously developed a system to promptly deactivate accounts involved in phishing, often before the victims could respond. The shutting down of the warez scene on AOL caused most phishers to leave the service, and many phishers—often young teens—grew out of the habit.

AOL Account Information

Capture of AOL account information may have led phishers to misuse credit card information, which then evolved into attacks against online payment systems. The first known direct attempt against a payment system affected E-gold in June 2001, which was followed up by a "post-911 id check" shortly after the September 11 attacks on the World Trade Center. Both were viewed at the time as failures, but can now be seen as early experiments towards more fruitful attacks against mainstream banks. By 2004, phishing was recognised as fully industrialised, in the sense of an economy of crime: specialisations emerged on a global scale and provided components for cash which were assembled into a finished attack.

More recent phishing attempts have targeted the customers of banks and online payment services. E-mails supposedly from the Internal Revenue Service have also been used to glean sensitive data from U.S. taxpayers. While the first such examples were sent indiscriminately in the hope of finding a customer of a given bank or service, recent research has shown that phishers may in principle be able to establish what bank a potential victim has a relationship with, and then send an appropriate spoofed email to this victim. Targeted versions of phishing have been termed spear phishing. Social networking sites are also a target of phishing, since the personal details in such sites can be used in identity theft; in late 2006 a computer worm took over pages on MySpace and altered links to direct surfers to websites designed to steal login details. Experiments show a success rate of over 70% for phishing attacks on social networks.

Phishing Techniques

Most methods of phishing use some form of technical deception designed to make a link in an email (and the spoofed website it leads to) appear to belong to the spoofed organisation. Misspelled URLs or the use of subdomains are common tricks used by phishers, such as this example URL, http://www.yourbank.com.example.com/. Another common trick is to make the anchor text for a link appear to be valid, when the link actually goes to the phishers' site.

An old method of spoofing used links containing the '@' symbol, originally intended as a way to include a username and password (contrary to the standard). Such URLs were disabled in Internet Explorer, while the Mozilla and Opera web browsers opted to present a warning message and give the option of continuing to the site or cancelling. A further problem with URLs has been found in the handling of Internationalised domain names (IDN) in web browsers, that might allow visually identical web addresses to lead to different, possibly malicious, websites.

Despite the publicity surrounding the flaw, known as IDN spoofing or a homograph attack, no known phishing attacks have yet taken advantage of it. Phishers have taken advantage of a similar risk, using open URL redirectors on the websites of trusted organisations to disguise malicious URLs with a trusted domain.

Filter evasion

Phishers have used images instead of text to make it harder for anti-phishing filters to detect text commonly used in phishing emails.

Once the victim visits the website the deception is not over. Some phishing scams use JavaScript commands in order to alter the address bar. This is done either by placing a picture of a legitimate URL over the address bar, or by closing the original address bar and opening a new one with the legitimate URL.

An attacker can even use flaws in a trusted website's own scripts against the victim. These types of attacks (known as cross-site scripting) are particularly problematic, because they direct the user to sign in at their bank or service's own web page, where everything from the web address to the security certificates appears correct. In reality, the link to the website is crafted to carry out the attack, although it is very difficult to spot without specialist knowledge. Just such a flaw was used in 2006 against PayPal.

A Universal Man-in-the-middle Phishing Kit, discovered by RSA Security, provides a simple-to-use interface that allows a phisher to convincingly reproduce websites and capture log-in details entered at the fake site.

Not all phishing attacks require a fake website. Messages that claimed to be from a bank told users to dial a phone number regarding problems with their bank accounts. Once the phone number (owned by the phisher, and provided by a Voice over IP service) was dialed, prompts told users to enter their account numbers and PIN. Voice phishing sometimes uses fake caller-ID data to give the appearance that calls come from a trusted organisation.

In an example PayPal phish (right), spelling mistakes in the email and the presence of an IP address in the link (visible in the tooltip under the yellow box) are both clues that this is a phishing attempt. Another giveaway is the lack of a personal greeting, although the presence of personal details is not a guarantee of legitimacy.

Damage Caused by Phishing Ranges

The damage caused by phishing ranges from loss of access to email to substantial financial loss. This style of identity theft is becoming more popular, because of the ease with which unsuspecting people often divulge personal information to phishers, including credit card numbers, social security numbers, and mothers' maiden names. There are also fears that identity thieves can add such information to the knowledge they gain simply by accessing public records. Once this information is acquired, the phishers may use a person's details to create fake accounts in a victim's name, ruin a victim's credit, or even prevent victims from accessing their own accounts.

It is estimated that between May 2004 and May 2005, approximately 1.2 million computer users in the United States suffered losses caused by phishing, totaling approximately US$929 million. U.S. businesses lose an estimated US$2 billion per year as their clients become victims. In the United Kingdom losses from web banking fraud—mostly from phishing—almost doubled to £23.2m in 2005, from £12.2m in 2004, while 1 in 20 users claimed to have lost out to phishing in 2005.

The UK banking body APACS' stance is that "customers must also take sensible precautions...so that they are not vulnerable to the criminal." Similarly, when the first spate of phishing attacks hit the Irish Republic's banking sector in September 2006, the Bank of Ireland initially refused to (and still insists that its policy is not to) cover losses suffered by its customers, although losses to the tune of •11300 were made good.

Anti-phishing Techniques

There are several different techniques to combat phishing, including legislation and technology created specifically to protect against phishing.

Social responses

One strategy for combating phishing is to train users to deal with phishing attempts. User education can be promising, especially where training provides direct feedback to the user on his success (or otherwise). One newer phishing tactic, which uses phishing emails targeted at a specific company, known as spear phishing, has been harnessed to train users at various locations, including West Point Military Academy. In a June 2004 experiment with spear phishing, 80% of 500 West Point cadets who were sent a fake email were tricked into revealing personal information.

Users can take steps to avoid phishing attempts by slightly modifying their browsing habits. Users who are contacted about an account needing to be "verified" (or any other topic used by phishers) can contact the company that is the subject of the email to check that the email is legitimate, or can type in a trusted web address for the company's website into the address bar of their browser to bypass the link in the suspected phishing message.

Nearly all legitimate email messages from companies to their customers will contain an item of information that is not readily available to phishers. Some companies, like PayPal, always address their customers by their username in emails, so if an email addresses a user in a generic fashion ("Dear PayPal customer") it is likely to be an attempt at phishing. Emails from banks and credit card companies will often include partial account numbers. However, recent research has shown that typical users do not distinguish between the first few digits and the last few digits of an account number. This is a significant problem since the first few digits often are the same for all clients of one financial institution. One should always be suspicious if the message does not contain specific personal information.

Phishing attempts in early 2006, however, used such highly personalised information, making it unsafe to rely on personal information alone as a sign that a message is legitimate. Furthermore, another recent study concluded in part that the presence of this information does not significantly affect the success rate of phishing attacks, suggesting that most users do not pay attention to such details anyway.

The Anti-Phishing Working Group, an industry and law enforcement association, has suggested that conventional phishing techniques could become obsolete in the future as people are increasingly aware of the social engineering techniques used by phishers. They propose that pharming and other uses of malware will become more common tools for stealing information.

Technical responses

Anti-phishing measures have been implemented as features embedded in browsers, as extensions or toolbars for browsers, and as part of website login procedures. The following are some of the main approaches to the problem.

Helping users identify legitimate sites: Since phishing is based on impersonation, preventing it depends on users having some reliable way to identify the sites they are dealing with. For example, some anti-phishing toolbars display the real domain name for the visited website. The petname extension for Firefox lets users type in their own labels for websites, so they can later recognise when they are back at the correct site. If the site is a suspect, then the software may either warn the user or block the site outright.

Alerting users to fraudulent websites: Another popular approach to fighting phishing is to maintain a list of known phishing sites and to check websites against the list. Microsoft's IE7 browser, Mozilla Firefox 2.0, and Opera all contain this type of anti-phishing measure. Firefox 2 uses Google anti-phishing software. Opera 9.1 uses live blacklists from PhishTank and GeoTrust, as well as live whitelists from GeoTrust. Some implementations of this approach send the visited URLs to a central service to be checked, which has raised concerns about compromising the user's privacy. According to a report by Mozilla in late 2006, Firefox 2 was found to be more effective than Internet Explorer 7 at detecting fraudulent sites in a study by an independent software testing company.

An approach introduced in mid-2006 involves switching to a special DNS service that filters out known phishing domains, which will work with any browser. This is similar in principle to using a hosts file to block web adverts. To mitigate the problem of phishing sites spoofing a victim site and embedding its images (such as logos) in a spoof site, several site owners have responded by altering the images to send a message to the visitor. If the images were not requested in the normal way by visiting the real page then a warning that the site is fraudulent can be substituted for the usual image, or the original image can be moved to a new filename and the original permanently replaced with a warning.

Augmenting password logins: Bank of America is one of several websites that ask users to select a personal image, and display this user-selected image with any forms that request a password. Users are instructed to only enter a password when they see the image they selected; if the correct image does not appear, they are expected to recognise that the site is not legitimate. However, a recent study suggests few users refrain from entering their password when images are absent. This feature (like other forms of two-factor authentication) is also susceptible to other attacks, such as those suffered by Scandinavian bank Nordea in late 2005, and Citibank in 2006.

Security skins are a related technique that involves overlaying a user-selected image across the login form as a visual cue that the form is legitimate. However, unlike the website-based image schemes, this image is shared between the user and the browser, not between the user and the website. The scheme also relies on a mutual authentication protocol, which makes it less vulnerable to attacks that affect user-only authentication schemes.

Eliminating phishing mail: Spam filters can also help by reducing the number of phishing emails that users receive in their inboxes.

Monitoring and takedown

Several companies offer banks and other entities likely to suffer from phishing scams 24/7 services to monitor, analyse and assist in shutting down phishing websites.

Individuals can contribute by reporting phishing to both volunteer and industry groups, such as PhishTank.

Legal responses

On January 26, 2004, the U.S. Federal Trade Commission filed the first lawsuit against a suspected phisher. The defendant, a Californian teenager, allegedly created and used a webpage designed to look like the America Online website, so that he could steal credit card information. Other countries have followed the lead of the U.S. by tracing and arresting phishers. A phishing kingpin, Valdir Paulo de Almeida, was arrested in Brazil for leading one of the largest phishing crime rings, which in 2 years stole between $18 and $37 million USD. UK authorities jailed two men in June 2005 for their role in a phishing scam, in a case connected to the U.S. Secret Service Operation Firewall, which targeted notorious "carder" websites. In 2006 eight people were arrested by Japanese police on suspicion of phishing fraud by creating bogus Yahoo Japan Web sites, netting themselves 100 million yen ($870 thousand USD). The arrests continued in 2006 with the FBI Operation Cardkeeper detaining a gang of sixteen in the U.S. and Europe.

In the United States, Senator Patrick Leahy introduced the Anti-Phishing Act of 2005 on March 1, 2005. The federal anti-phishing bill proposes that criminals who create fake web sites and spam bogus emails in order to defraud consumers could receive a fine up to $250,000 and receive jail terms of up to five years. The UK strengthened the legal arsenal against phishing with the Fraud Act 2006, which introduces a general offence of fraud that can carry up to a ten year sentence, and prohibits writing or possessing phishing kits with intent to commit fraud.

Companies have also joined the effort to crack down on phishing. On March 31, 2005, Microsoft filed 117 federal lawsuits in the U.S. District Court for the Western District of Washington. The lawsuits accuse "John Doe" defendants of using various methods to obtain passwords and confidential information. March 2005 also saw Microsoft partner with the Australian government to teach law enforcement officials how to combat various cyber crimes, including phishing. Microsoft announced a planned further 100 lawsuits outside the U.S. in March 2006, followed by the commencement, as of November 2006, of 129 lawsuits mixing criminal and civil actions.

AOL reinforced its efforts against phishing in early 2006 with three lawsuits seeking a total of $18 million USD under the 2005 amendments to the Virginia Computer Crimes Act, and Earthlink has joined in by helping to identify six men subsequently charged with phishing fraud in Connecticut.

6

Web-based E-mail

Web-based email or webmail is a term referring to an e-mail service intended to be primarily accessed via a web browser, as opposed to through an application such as Mozilla's Thunderbird, Apple's Mail or Microsoft Outlook.

One of the earliest Webmail services was Hotmail. Now, the most popular Webmail providers are arguably Gmail and Yahoo! Mail.

A major advantage of web-based email over application-based email is that a user has the ability to access their inbox from any Internet-connected computer. However, the need for Internet access is also a setback, in that one cannot access their old messages, or work on new ones, when they are not connected to the Internet.

In 1997, prior to its acquisition by Microsoft, Hotmail introduced its service, which became one of the first popular web-based email offerings. Following Hotmail's initial success, Yahoo! released their webmail service, which also grew to become widely popular.

Google's introduction of Gmail in 2004 sparked a period of rapid development in webmail, due to Gmail's new features such as JavaScript menus, text-based ads, and massive storage. Other webmail providers responded by offering similar features, such as Yahoo!'s introduction of its new version of Yahoo! Mail.

Software Packages

There are also software packages that allow an organisation such as company to offer email through the web for their associates. Some solutions are open source software like SquirrelMail and others are closed source like the Outlook Web Access module for Microsoft Exchange, Socketmail and Atmail.

Conversely, there are programmes that can simulate a web browser to access webmail as if it were stored in a POP3 or IMAP account. They are susceptible, though, to changes in the user interface of the web service since there is no standard interface.

Rendering and Compatibility

There are important differences in rendering capabilities for many popular webmail services such as Gmail, Windows Live Hotmail, and Yahoo Mail. Due to the various treatment of HTML tags, such as <style> and <head>, as well as CSS rendering inconsistencies, email marketing companies rely on older web development techniques to send cross-platform mail. This usually means a heavy reliance on tables and inline stylesheets.

Domain Name System

The term domain name has multiple related meanings:

— A name that identifies a computer or computers on the internet. These names appear as a component of a Web site's URL, e.g. wikipedia.org. This type of domain name is also called a hostname.

— The product that domain name registrars provide to their customers. These names are often called registered domain names.

— Names used for other purposes in the Domain Name System (DNS), for example the special name which follows the @ sign in an email address, or the Top-level domains like.com, or the names used by the Session Initiation Protocol (VoIP), or DomainKeys.

— They are sometimes colloquially (and incorrectly) referred to by marketers as "web addresses".

The most common types of domain names are hostnames that provide more memorable names to stand in for numeric IP addresses. They allow for any service to move to a different location in the topology of the Internet (or an intranet), which would then have a different IP address.

By allowing the use of unique alphabetical addresses instead of numeric ones, domain names allow Internet users to more easily find and communicate with web sites and other server-based services.

The flexibility of the domain name system allows multiple IP addresses to be assigned to a single domain name, or multiple domain names to be assigned to a single IP address. This means that one server may have multiple roles (such as hosting multiple independent Web sites), or that one role can be spread among many servers. One IP address can also be assigned to several servers, as used in anycast and hijacked IP space.

Hostnames are restricted to the ASCII letters "a" through "z" (case-insensitive), the digits "0" through "9", and the hyphen, with some other restrictions. Registrars restrict the domains to valid hostnames, since, otherwise, they would be useless. The Internationalised domain name (IDN) system has been developed to bypass the restrictions on character allowances in hostnames, making it easier for users of non-english alphabets to use the Internet. The underscore character is frequently used to ensure that a domain name is not recognised as a hostname, for example with the use of SRV records, although some older systems, such as NetBIOS did allow it. Due to confusion and other reasons, domain names with underscores in them are sometimes used where hostnames are required.

Top-level Domains

Every domain name ends in a top-level domain (TLD) name, which is always either one of a small list of generic names (three or more characters), or a two-character territory code based on ISO-3166 (there are few exceptions and new codes are integrated case by case). Top-level domains are sometimes also called first-level domains.

In addition to the top-level domains, there are second-level domain (SLD) names. These are the names directly to the left of.com,.net, and the other top-level domains. On the next level are third-level domains. These domains are immediately to the left of a second-level domain. In the example, "en" is a third-level domain. There can be fourth and fifth level domains and so on, with virtually no limitation.

Domains of third or higher level are also known as subdomains, though this term technically applies to a domain of any level, since even a top-level domain is a "subdomain" of the "root" domain (a "zeroth-level" domain that is designated by a dot alone).

Traditionally, the second level domain was the name of the company or the name used on the internet. The third level was commonly used to designate a particular host server. Therefore, ftp.wikipedia.org might be an FTP server, www.wikipedia.org would be a World Wide Web

Server, and mail.wikipedia.org could be an email server. Modern technology now allows multiple servers to serve a single subdomain, or multiple protocols or domains to be served by a single computer. Therefore, subdomains may or may not have any real purpose.

Official Assignment

ICANN (Internet Corporation for Assigned Names and Numbers) has overall responsibility for managing the DNS. It controls the root domain, delegating control over each top-level domain to a domain name registry. For ccTLDs, the domain registry is typically controlled by the government of that country. ICANN has a consultation role in these domain registries but is in no position to regulate the terms and conditions of how a domain name is allocated or who allocates it in each of these country level domain registries. On the other hand, generic top-level domains (gTLDs) are governed directly under ICANN which means all terms and conditions are defined by ICANN with the cooperation of the gTLD registries.

Domain names which are theoretically leased can be considered in the same way as real estate, due to a significant impact on online brand building, advertising, search engine optimization, etc.

A few companies have offered low-cost, below-cost or even free domain registrations, with a variety of models adopted to recoup the costs to the provider. These usually require that domains are hosted on their site in a framework or portal, with advertising wrapped around the user's content, revenue from which allows the provider to recoup the costs. When the DNS was new, domain registrations were free.

Uses and Abuses

As domain names became attractive to marketers, rather

than just the technical audience for which they were originally intended, they began to be used in manners that in many cases did not fit in their intended structure.

As originally planned, the structure of domain names followed a strict hierarchy in which the top level domain indicated the type of organisation (commercial, governmental, etc.), and addresses would be nested down to third, fourth, or further levels to express complex structures, where, for instance, branches, departments, and subsidiaries of a parent organisation would have addresses which were subdomains of the parent domain. Also, hostnames were intended to correspond to actual physical machines on the network, generally with only one name per machine.

However, once the World Wide Web became popular, site operators frequently wished to have memorable addresses, regardless of whether they fit properly in the structure; thus, since the.com domain was the most popular and memorable, even noncommercial sites would often get addresses under it, and sites of all sorts wished to have second-level domain registrations even if they were parts of a larger entity where a logical subdomain would have made sense.

A Web site found at http://www.example.org/ will often be advertised without the "http://", and in most cases can be reached by just entering "example.org" into a Web browser. In the case of a.com, the Web site can sometimes be reached by just entering "example".

The popularity of domain names also led to uses which were regarded as abusive by established companies with trademark rights; this was known as cybersquatting, in which somebody took a name that resembled a trademark in order to profit from traffic to that address. To combat this, various laws and policies were enacted to allow abusive registrations to be forcibly transferred, but these were sometimes themselves abused by overzealous companies committing reverse domain hijacking against domain users who had legitimate grounds to hold their names, such as their being generic words as well as trademarks in a particular context, or their use in the context of fan or protest sites with free speech rights of their own.

Laws that specifically address domain name conflicts include the Anticybersquatting Consumer Protection Act in the United States and the Trademarks Act, 1999, in India. Alternatively, domain registrants are bound by contract under the UDRP to comply with mandatory arbitration proceedings should someone challenge their ownership of the domain name.

Generic Domain Names

Within a particular top-level domain, parties are generally free to select an unallocated domain name as their own on a first come, first served basis, resulting in Harris's lament, all the good ones are taken. For generic or commonly used names, this may sometimes lead to the use of a domain name which is inaccurate or misleading. This problem can be seen with regard to the ownership or control of domain names for a generic product or service.

By way of illustration, there has been tremendous growth in the number and size of literary festivals around the world in recent years. In this context, currently a generic domain name such as literary.org is available to the first literary festival organisation which is able to obtain registration, even if the festival in question is very young or obscure. Some critics would argue that there is greater amenity in reserving such domain names for the use of, for example, a regional or umbrella grouping of festivals. Related issues may also arise in relation to non-commercial domain names.

Unconventional domain names

Due to the rarity of one-word dot-com domain names, many unconventional domain names, domain hacks, have been gaining popularity. They make use of the top-level domain as an integral part of the Web site's title. Two popular domain hack Web sites are del.icio.us and blo.gs, which spell out "delicious" and "blogs", respectively.

Unconventional domain names are also used to create unconventional email addresses. Non-working examples that spell 'James' are j@m.es and j@mes.com, which use the domain names m.es (of Spain's.es) and mes.com, respectively.

Commercial resale of domain names

An economic effect of the widespread usage of domain names has been the resale market (after-market) for generic domain names that has sprung up in the last decade. Certain domains, especially those related to business, gambling, pornography, and other commercially lucrative fields of digital world trade have become very much in demand to corporations and entrepreneurs due to their importance in attracting clients.

The most expensive Internet domain name to date, according to Guinness World Records, is business.com which was resold in 1999 for $7.5 million, but this was $7.5 million in stock options, not in cash. The stock was later redeemed for $2 million, "So it was $2 million.". There are disputes about the high values of domain names claimed and the actual cash prices of many sales such Business.com.

Another high-priced domain name, sex.com, was stolen from its rightful owner by means of a forged transfer instruction via fax. During the height of the dot-com era, the domain was earning millions of dollars per month in advertising revenue from the large influx of visitors that arrived daily.

The sex.com sale may have never been final as the domain is still with the previous owner. Also, that sale was not just a domain but an income stream, a web site, a domain name with customers and advertisers, etc. Two long-running U.S. lawsuits resulted, one against the thief and one against the domain registrar VeriSign.

In one of the cases, Kremen v. Network Solutions, the court found in favor of the plaintiff, leading to an unprecedented ruling that classified domain names as property, granting them the same legal protections. In 1999, Microsoft traded the name Bob.com with internet entrepreneur Bob Kerstein for the name Windows2000.com which was the name of their new operating system.

One of the reasons for the value of domain names is that even without advertising or marketing, they attract clients seeking services and products who simply type in the generic name. Furthermore, generic domain names such as movies.com or Books.com are extremely easy for potential customers to remember, increasing the probability that they become repeat customers or regular clients.

Although the current domain market is nowhere as strong as it was during the dot-com heyday, it remains strong and is currently experiencing solid growth again. Annually tens of millions of dollars change hands due to the resale of domains. Large numbers of registered domain names lapse and are deleted each year. On average 25,000 domain names drop (are deleted) every day.

It is very important to remember that a domain (name, address) must be valued separately from the website (content, revenue) that it is used for. The high prices have usually been paid for the revenue that was generated from the website at the domain's address (url.). The intrinsic value of a domain is the registration fee. There is no such a thing as a current market value for a domain: It just takes what somebody pays.

The Fair Market Value of a domain can be anything from the registration fee: The lowest known past selling price, the highest known past selling, price, the most recent selling price, or just any past selling price and any of these (or any sum resp. division etc.) is usually added to the current or expected revenue from the web content (advertising, sales, etc.).

Domain (name + ext.) should not be mixed with website (content + revenue). The estimation by appraisers are always the addition of what they would like that a domain is worth together with the effective/expected/desired revenue from the web content. Some people put value on the length of the SLD (name) and other people prefer description capability, but the shorter a SLD is, the less descriptive it can be.

Also, if short is crucial, then the TLD (extension) should be short too. It is less realistic to get a domain like LL.travel or LL.mobi than a domain travel.LL or mobi.LL. This illustrates the relativity of domain value estimation. It can be safely put that the revenue af a web (content) can be easily stated, but that the value of a domain (SLD.TLD aka name.ext) is a matter of opinions and preferences. In the end, however, any sale depend of the estimates by the domain seller and the domain buyer.

People who buy and sell domain names are known as domainers. People who sell value estimation services are known as appraisers.

According to Guiness Book of World Records and MSNBC, the most expensive domain name sales on record as of 2004 were: Business.com for $7.5 million in December 1999, AsSeenOnTv.com for $5.1 million in January 2000, Altavista.com for $3.3 million in August 1998, Wine.com for $2.9 million in September 1999, CreditCards.com for $2.75 million in July 2004, and Autos.com for $2.2 million in December 1999.

7

Disposable E-mail Address

Disposable e-mail addressing (DEA) refers to an alternative way of sharing and managing e-mail addressing. DEA aims to set up a new, unique e-mail address for every contact or entity, making a point-to-point connection between the sender and the recipient. Subsequently, if anyone compromises the address or utilises it in connection with any e-mail abuse, the address-owner can easily cancel (or "dispose" of) it without affecting any other contact. Following the cancellation or replacement of a disposable e-mail address, the (ex-)owner need notify no more than one person/contact of the change.

Disposable e-mail addressing, in essence, sets up a different, unique DEA for every sender/recipient combination. It operates most usefully in situations where someone may sell or release an e-mail address to spam lists or to other unscrupulous entities. The most common situations of this type involve online registrations for things such as discussion groups, bulletin boards, chat rooms, online shopping, and file hosting services. In a time when e-mail spam has become an everyday nuisance, and when identity theft threatens, DEAs can serve as a convenient tool for keeping network users safe and sane.

Most likely, but not always, cancellation of a disposable e-mail address takes place because someone starts to use the address in an illegitimate manner. This may occur through the accidental release of an e-mail to a spam list, or because the original recipient unscrupulously and deliberately obtained it deceptively. Alternatively, the user may simply decide not to receive further correspondence from that company. Whatever the cause, DEA allows the address owner to take unilateral action by simply cancelling the address in question. Later, the owner can determine whether to update the recipient or not.

For the sake of convenience, disposable e-mail addresses typically forward to one or more real e-mail mailboxes where the owner receives and reads messages. The contact with whom a DEA is shared never needs to know the real e-mail address of the user. If a database manages the DEA, it can also quickly identify the expected sender of each message by retrieving the associated contact name of each unique DEA. Used properly, DEA can also help identify which recipients handle e-mail addresses in a careless or illegitimate manner. Moreover, it can serve as an effective tool for spotting counterfeit messages, or phishers.

Advantages over Traditional E-mail

Ideally, owners share a DEA once with each contact/ entity. Thus, if the DEA should ever change, only one entity needs to be updated. By comparison, the traditional practice of giving the same e-mail address to multiple recipients means that if that address subsequently changes, many legitimate recipients will need to receive notification of the change and to update their records—a potentially tedious process.

Additionally, because access has been narrowed down to one contact, that entity then becomes the most likely point of compromise for any spam that account receives. This allows users to determine first hand the trustworthiness of the people they share their DEAs with. "Safe" DEAs that have not been abused can be forwarded to a real e-mail account, while messages sent to "compromised" DEAs can be routed to a special folder, sent to the trash, held for spam filtering, or returned undeliverable if the DEA is deleted outright.

Further, because DEAs serve as a layer of indirection between the sender and recipient, if the DEA user's actual email address changes, for instance moving from a university address to a local ISP, then the user need only update the DEA service provider of the change, and all outstanding DEAs will continue to function without updating.

Security and Filtering

It is possible for spammers to "guess" commonly used DEAs by trying addresses in the form of <Common CompanyName@RandomName.DEAServiceProvider.com> or other widely used formats. This is especially likely if a user's subdomain (The "RandomName" part) has already been posted publicly somewhere. To combat this, users can make their e-mail addresses more obscure through using random names, checksums, a mutated form of a name, or some combination of the above.

A harder-to-guess example might be <Company Name.Checksum@YourDomain.DEAServiceProvider.com> or<RandomTextCompanyNameRandomText@YourDomain.DEA ServiceProvider.com>. There is an obvious tradeoff in that the more obscure an address is, the harder it will be for users to remember and quickly type them. Mentally computed checksums may help with this.

"Poor man's DEA"

The plus addressing technique allows users to create DEAs using an existing e-mail address without the need for a DEA service provider. All that is required is for the e-mail server to support plus addressing. A checkstring, which is optional, allows the MTA to block attempts by spammers to bypass the DEA filtering. As an example, a static string or checksum that can be computed in one's head (or by a MTA with sieve or procmail) can be used as a checkstring that can be added to a DEA to evade spammers.

As an example, <User+CompanyName. Check String@EmailServiceProvider.com> can function as a hard-to-compromise "poor man's DEA". It is possible for a human (or a programme) to extract the real e-mail address just by removing everything after the plus; however it is considered unlikely that a programme would bother going to this effort, since the vast majority of e-mail addresses do not use this technique.

Downside

Many forum and wiki administrators dislike DEAs because they obfuscate the identity of the members and make maintaining member control harder. As an example, trolls and vandals like to use throwaway e-mail addresses to get around attempts to ban them. Using a DEA provider only makes this easier; the same convenience with which a person may create a DEA to filter spam also applies to trolls. For this reason, most forum programmes have functionality to make it easier to ban DEAs. As a result, forum, wiki administrators, blog owners, and indeed any public site requiring user names may have a compelling reason to ban DEAs.

As a counterbalance to the risks of asking a user to give a "permanent" e-mail address in a publicly accessible site, administrators have the option to prevent, or give the option for hiding, the publication of users' email addresses. An "e-mail this user" script can be used to allow communication with the user without the sender knowing their e-mail address. This protects users from spam and allows them to use real email addresses, which may make a ban on DEAs easier for users to accept.

Caught in the crossfire between Internet undesirables and administrative attempts to deal with them, DEA providers have trouble presenting a total solution. A user may find it advantageous to decide whether to provide a "real" e-mail address to a public/commercial entity on a case-by-case basis. On the one side, the trustworthiness and reputation of the site administrators, the availability of options to hide e-mail addresses, and the existence/enforcement of an acceptable privacy policy are all factors that should be taken into account. On the other, there are the risks of confusing people by using long or oddly named addresses often associated with DEAs, being perceived as a troll or someone with a motive to hide their identity, and the chance that the DEA provider may eventually cease operations.

E-mail Address

An e-mail address identifies a location to which e-mail messages can be delivered. The term "e-mail address" is also used as the formal pre-registered authoritative electronic mailing delivery site for an individual (example: an attorney's e-mail address registered for delivery of proof of service digital copies of legal pleadings). A modern Internet e-mail address (using SMTP or Usenet) is a string of the form jsmith@example.com. It should be read as "jsmith at example dot com". The part before the @ sign is the local-part of the address, often the username of the recipient, and the part after the @ sign is the domain-part which may be a host name or domain name which can be looked up in the Domain Name System to find the mail transfer agent or Mail eXchangers (MXs) accepting e-mail for that address.

The domain name of an e-mail address is often that of the e-mail service, such as Google's Gmail, Microsoft's Hotmail, etc. The domain name can also be the domain name of the company that the recipient represents, or the domain of the recipient's personal site.

Earlier forms of e-mail addresses included the somewhat verbose notation required by X.400, and the UUCP "bang path" notation, in which the address was given in the form of a sequence of computers through which the message should be relayed. This latter was widely used for several years, but was superseded by the generally more convenient SMTP form.

Addresses found in the header fields of e-mail should not be considered authoritative, because SMTP has no generally-required mechanisms for authentication. Forged e-mail addresses are often seen in spam, phishing, and many other internet-based scams; this has led to several initiatives which aim to make such forgeries easier to spot.

Limitations

The format of Internet e-mail addresses is defined in RFC 2822, which permits them to consist of only a subset of ASCII characters.

As defined in RFC 2821, the local-part of an e-mail address has a maximum of 64 characters (although servers are encouraged to not limit themselves to accepting only 64 characters) and the domain name a maximum of 255 characters. Unlike everything else in the header, the local-part "MUST BE treated as case sensitive. [...] However, exploiting the case sensitivity of mailbox local-parts impedes interoperability and is discouraged."

Local part is the portion of a mail address before the @ character. This normally identifies a particular mailbox within a site mail system so is not usually of interest to other mail systems.

According to RFC 2822, the local-part of the address may use any of these ASCII characters:

— Uppercase and lowercase letters (case sensitive)

— The digits 0 through 9

— The characters ! # $ % * / ? | ^ { } ' ~ & ' + - = _

— The character. provided that it is not the first or last character in the local-part.

Additionally, RFC 2821 and RFC 2822 allow the local-part to be a quoted-string, as in "John Doe"@example.com, thus allowing characters in the local-part that would otherwise be prohibited. However, RFC 2821 warns: "a host that expects to receive mail SHOULD avoid defining mailboxes where the Local-part requires (or uses) the Quoted-string form".

Not with standing the addresses permitted by these standards, some systems impose more restrictions on email addresses, both in email addresses created on the system and in email addresses to which messages can be sent. Hotmail, for example, only allows creation of email addresses using alphanumerics, dot (.), underscore (_) and hyphen (-), and will not allow sending mail to any email address containing ! # $ % * / ? | ^ { } ' ~.

The domain name is much more restricted. The dot separated domain labels are limited to "letters, digits, and hyphens drawn from the ASCII character set... Mailbox domains are not case sensitive." The informational RFC 3696 written by the author of RFC 2821 explains the details in a readable way, with a few minor errors noted in the 3696 errata.

Plus (or Minus) Addressing

According to RFC 2821 2.3.10 Mailbox and Address, "...the local-part MUST be interpreted and assigned semantics only by the host specified in the domain part of the address.". In particular, for some hosts the user "smith" is different from the user "Smith". Plus addressing is one of the benefits of this limitation. Some mail servers allow a user to append +tag to their email address (joeuser+tag@example.com). Some systems violate RFC 2822, and the recommendations in RFC 3696, by refusing to send mail addressed to a user on another system merely because the local-part of the address contains the plus sign (+). Users of these systems cannot use plus addressing.

On the other hand, most qmail installations support the use of a dash '-' as a separator between local-address and domain parts. Such as joeuser-tag@example.com or joeuser-tag-sub-anything-else@example.com. This allows qmail through.qmail-default or.qmail-tag-sub-anything-else files to sort, filter, forward, or run application based on the tagging system established. Procmail and Spam Assassin are common applications to use with qmail to help sort out spam or further filter incoming email.

8

Simple Mail Transfer Protocol

Simple Mail Transfer Protocol (SMTP) is the defacto standard for e-mail transmissions across the Internet. The protocol used today is also known as ESMTP and defined in RFC 2821.

SMTP is a relatively simple, text-based protocol, where one or more recipients of a message are specified (and in most cases verified to exist) and then the message text is transferred. It is a client-server protocol, where the client transmits an email message to the server. Either an end-user's email client, a.k.a. MUA (Mail User Agent), or a relaying server's MTA (Mail Transfer Agents) can act as an SMTP client.

An email client knows the outgoing mail SMTP server from its configuration. A relaying server typically determines which SMTP server to connect to by looking up the MX (Mail eXchange) DNS record for each recipient's domain name (the part of the email address to the right of the at (@) sign). Conformant MTAs (not all) fall back to a simple A record in the case of no MX. Some current mail transfer agents will also use SRV records, a more general form of MX, though these are not widely adopted.

The SMTP client initiates a TCP connection to server's port 25 (unless overridden by configuration). It is quite easy to test an SMTP server using the telnet programme. SMTP is a "push" protocol that does not allow one to "pull" messages from a remote server on demand. To do this a mail client must use POP3 or IMAP. Another SMTP server can trigger a delivery in SMTP using ETRN.

Forms of one-to-one electronic messaging were used in the 1960s. People communicated with one another using systems developed for a particular mainframe computer. As more computers began to be interconnected with others, especially in the US Government's ARPANET, standards were developed to allow users using different systems to be able to email one another. SMTP grew out of these standards developed during the 1970s.

SMTP can trace its roots to the Mail Box Protocol (ca. 1971), FTP Mail (ca. 1973), and Mail Protocol. The work continued throughout the 1970s, until the ARPANET converted into the modern Internet around 1980. Jon Postel then proposed a Mail Transfer Protocol in 1980 that began to remove the mail's reliance on FTP. SMTP was published as RFC 821 in 1982, also by Jonathan Postel.

The SMTP standard was developed around the same time the Usenet was, a one-to-many communication network with some similarities. SMTP became widely used in the early 1980s. At the time, it was a complement to UUCP (Unix to Unix CoPy) mail, which was better suited to handle e-mail transfers between machines that were intermittently connected. SMTP, on the other hand, works best when both the sending and receiving machines are connected to the network all the time. Both use a store and forward mechanism and are examples of push technology. Usenet's news groups are still propagated with UUCP between servers, but UUCP mail has virtually disappeared along with the "bang paths" it used as message routing headers.

Sendmail was one of the first (if not the first) mail transfer agents to implement SMTP. Some other popular SMTP server programmes include Postfix, qmail, Novell GroupWise, Exim, Novell NetMail, Microsoft Exchange Server and Sun Java System Messaging Server. As of 2001 there were at least 50 programmes that implemented SMTP either as clients (senders of messages) or as servers (receivers of messages).

Message Submission (RFC 2576) and SMTP-AUTH (RFC 2554) were introduced in 1998 and 1999, both describing new trends in email delivery. Originally, SMTP servers were typically internal to an organisation, receiving mail for the organisation from the outside, and relaying messages from the organisation to the outside. But as time went on, SMTP servers (Mail transfer agents), in practice, were expanding their roles to become Mail submission agents for Mail user agents, some of which were now relaying mail from the outside of an organisation. This issue, a consequence of the rapid expansion and popularity of the World Wide Web, meant that the SMTP protocol had to include specific rules and methods for relaying mail and authenticating users to prevent abuses such as unsolicited email (spam) relaying.

Since this protocol started out as purely ASCII text-based, it did not deal well with binary files. Standards such as Multipurpose Internet Mail Extensions (MIME) were developed to encode binary files for transfer through SMTP. MTAs developed after Sendmail also tended to be implemented 8-bit-clean, so that the alternate "just send eight" strategy could be used to transmit arbitrary data via SMTP. Non-8-bit-clean MTAs today tend to support the 8BITMIME extension, permitting binary files to be transmitted almost as easily as plain text.

Developers

Many people edited or contributed to the core SMTP specifications, among them Jon Postel, Eric Allman, Dave Crocker, Ned Freed, Randall Gellens, John Klensin, and Keith Moore.

Outgoing Mail SMTP Server

An email client requires the name or the IP address of an SMTP server as part of its configuration. The server will deliver messages on behalf of the user. This setting allows for various policies and network designs. End users connected to the Internet can use the services of an e-mail provider that is not necessarily the same as their connection provider. Network topology, or the location of a client within a network or outside of a network, is no longer a limiting factor for email submission or delivery. Modern SMTP servers typically use a client's credentials (authentication) rather than a client's location (IP address), to determine whether it is eligible to relay email.

Another choice is whether to use TCP port 25 (SMTP) or port 587 (Submission), as established by RFC 2476, for relaying outbound mail to a mail server. Many servers support both. Some servers still support port 465 for legacy secure SMTP, but it is preferable to use encryption on standard ports according to RFC 2487. Some servers are setup to reject all relaying on port 25, but valid users authenticating on port 587 are allowed to relay mail to any valid address. A server that relays all email for all destinations for all clients connecting to port 25 is known as an open relay and is generally considered a bad practice worthy of blacklisting.

Sample Communications

After establishing a connection between the sender (the

client) and the receiver (the server), the following is a legal SMTP session. In the following conversation, everything sent by the client is prefaced with C: and everything sent by the server is prefaced with S:. On most computer systems, a connection can be established using the telnet command on the client machine, for example.

telnet www.example.com 25

which opens a TCP connection from the sending machine to the MTA listening on port 25 on host www.example.com.

— S: 220 www.example.com ESMTP Postfix

— C: HELO mydomain.com

— S: 250 Hello mydomain.com

— C: MAIL FROM:<sender@mydomain.com>

— S: 250 Ok C: RCPT TO:<friend@example.com>

— S: 250 Ok

— C: DATA

— S: 354 End data with <CR><LF>.<CR><LF>

— C: Subject: test message

— C: From: sender@mydomain.com

— C: To: friend@example.com

— C:

— C: Hello,

— C: This is a test.

— C: Goodbye.

— C:. S: 250 Ok: queued as 12345

— C: QUIT

– S: 221 Bye

Contemporary clients will use the ESMTP extension keyword SIZE to inquire of the server the maximum message size that will be accepted. Older clients and servers will try to transfer huge messages that will be rejected after wasting the network resources, including a lot of connect time to dialup ISPs that are paid by the minute.

For the edit planning of giant files or sending with older clients, users can manually determine in advance the maximum size accepted by ESMTP servers. The user telnets as above, but substitutes "EHLO mydomain.com" for the HELO command line.

S: 220-serverdomain.com ESMTP {postfix version and date} S: 220 NO UCE. {etc., terms of service} C: EHLO mydomain.com S: 250-serverdomain.com Hello mydomain.com [127.0.0.1] S: 250-SIZE 14680064 S: 250-PIPELINING S: 250 HELP

This serverdomain.com declares that it will accept a fixed maximum message size no larger than 14,680,064 octets (8-bit bytes). Depending on the server's actual resource usage, it may be currently unable to accept a message this large. In the simplest case, an ESMTP server will declare a maximum SIZE with only the EHLO user interaction. If no number appears after the SIZE keyword, or if the current message limit must be exactly determined, the user can further interact by simulating the ESMTP header of a message with an estimated size.

Anti-spam Techniques

One of the limitations of the original SMTP is that it has no facility for authentication of senders. Therefore the

SMTP-AUTH extension was defined. However, the impracticalities of widespread SMTP-AUTH implementation and management means that E-mail spamming is not and cannot be addressed by it. Modifying SMTP extensively, or replacing it completely, is not believed to be practical, due to the network effects of the huge installed base of SMTP. Internet Mail 2000 is one such proposal for replacement.

Spam is enabled by several factors, including vendors implementing broken MTAs (that do not adhere to standards, and therefore make it difficult for other MTAs to enforce standards), security vulnerabilities within the operating system (often exacerbated by always-on broadband connections) that allow spammers to remotely control end-user PCs and cause them to send spam, and a regrettable lack of "intelligence" in many MTAs.

There are a number of proposals for sideband protocols that will assist SMTP operation. The Anti-Spam Research Group (ASRG) of the Internet Research Task Force (IRTF) is working on a number of E-mail authentication and other proposals for providing simple source authentication that is flexible, lightweight, and scalable. Recent Internet Engineering Task Force (IETF) activities include MARID (2004) leading to two approved IETF experiments in 2005, and DomainKeys Identified Mail in 2006.

Other Protocols

Email is "handed off" (pushed) from a client (MUA) to a mail server (MSA), usually using Simple Mail Transfer Protocol or IMAP. From there, the MSA delivers the mail to a MTA, usually running on the same machine. The MTA looks up the destination(s)'s MX records with a DNS lookup, and begins to relay (push) the message to the server on record via TCP port 25 and SMTP. Once the receiving MTA accepts the incoming message, it is delivered via Mail delivery agent to a server which is designed for local mail delivery. Once delivered to the local mail server, the mail is stored for batch retrieval by authenticated mail clients (MUAs).

Generally speaking, mail retrieval (pull) is performed using either a type of online folders (e.g. IMAP 4, a protocol that both delivers and organizes mail) or the older single repository format (e.g. POP3, the Post Office Protocol). Webmail clients may use either method, but the retrieval protocol is often not a formal standard. Some local mail servers and MUAs are capable of either push or pull mail retrieval.

9

Internet Fax

Internet fax uses the internet to receive and send faxes. Traditional faxing involves sending a scanned copy of a document (a facsimile) from one fax machine to another, over the phone network. Internet faxing (or "online faxing") is a general term which can refer to one of several methods of achieving this over the Internet - with a goal of both reduced costs and increased functionality over traditional faxing.

Depending on the specific method/implementation, advantages of using the internet can include

— no extra telephone line required for the fax

— paperless communication, integrated with email

— send and receive multiple faxes simultaneously

— reduction in phone costs

Traditional Fax

The traditional method for sending faxes over phone lines (PSTN)

Fax machine → Phoneline → Fax machine

A fax machine is an electronic instrument composed of a

scanner, a modem, and a printer. It transmits data in the form of pulses via a telephone line to a recipient, usually another fax machine, which then transforms these impulses into images, and prints them on paper. The traditional method requires a phone line, and only one fax can be sent or received at a time.

Computer Based Faxing

As modems became common, some computers were used to send faxes directly. Instead of printing a document, and then putting it in a fax machine - computer software allowed users to print directly to the software fax, and then send the fax using the modem. Receiving faxes was accomplished similarly.

Computer → Phone line → Fax machine

Fax Machine → Phone line → Computer

Disadvantages of receiving faxes this way are that the computer has to be turned on and running the fax software to receive any faxes.

Internet Fax Servers

The Internet has enabled development of several other methods of sending and receiving a fax. The more common method is an extension of computer-based faxing, and involves using a fax server/gateway to the Internet to convert between faxes and emails. It is often referred to as "fax to mail" or "mail to fax". This technology is more and more replacing the traditional fax machine because it offers the advantage of dispensing with the machine as well as the additional telephone line.

Reception:

Fax machine → Phone line → Fax gateway → email

message (over Internet) → computer email account . A fax is sent via the Public Switched Telephone Network (PSTN) on the fax server, which receives the fax and convertes it into PDF or TIFF format, according to the instructions of the user.

The fax is then transmitted to the Web server which posts it in the Web interface on the account of the subscriber, who is alerted of the reception by an email containing the fax in an attached file and sometimes by a message on his mobile phone.

Sending:

Computer → Internet → Fax gateway → Phone line → Fax machine

From his/her computer, in the supplier Web site, the user chooses the document she wants to send and the fax number of the recipient. When sending, the document is usually converted to PDF format and sent by the Web server to the fax server, which then transmits it to the recipient fax machine via the Standard Telephone Network. Then the user receives a confirmation that the sending was carried out, in his/her web interface and/or by email.

An Internet fax service allows one to send faxes from a computer via an Internet connection, thanks to a Web interface usually available on the supplier's Web site. This technology has many advantages:

— No fax machine: no maintenance, no paper, toner expenditure, possible repairs, etc.

— Mobility: All actions are done on the Web interface; the service is thus available from any computer connected to Internet, everywhere in the world.

— Confidentiality: The faxes are received directly on the account of the user; he is the only one who can access it. The received faxes are not likely to be lost any more or read by the wrong people.

— No installation of software or hardware: All actions are done on the Web interface of the supplier, on the account of the user.

— No telephone subscription for an additional line dedicated to the fax.

— Many faxes can be sent or received simultaneously, and faxes can be received while the computer is switched off.

Fax using Voice over IP

Making phone calls over the Internet (Voice over Internet Protocol, or VoIP) has become increasingly popular. Compressing fax signals is different from compressing voice signals, so a new standard (T.38) has been created for this. If the VoIP adapter and gateway are T.38 compliant, most fax machines can simply be plugged into the VoIP adapter instead of a regular phone line.

Fax machine → VoIP adapter → VoIP gateway → Phone line → Fax machine (or vice versa)

As with regular faxes, only one fax can be sent or received at a time.

Fax using Email

While the needs of computer-to-fax communications are well covered, the simplicity of quickly faxing a handwritten document combined with the advantages of email are not.

"iFax" (T.37) was designed for fax machines to directly communicate via email. Faxes are sent as e-mail attachments in a TIFF-F format.

— iFax machine → email message (over Internet) → computer email account

— iFax machine → email message (over Internet) → iFax machine (using email address)

A new fax machine (supporting iFax/T.37) is required, as well as a known email address for the sending and receiving machines. This has limited the standard's use, though a system for looking up a fax's email address based on its phone number is under development . To work with existing fax machines, all iFax machines support standard faxing (requiring a regular phone line). Alternatively, an iFax can be used in conjunction with a fax gateway.

Fax Mechine

Fax (short for facsimile, from Latin fac simile, "make similar", i.e. "make a copy") is a telecommunications technology used to transfer copies (facsimiles) of documents, especially using affordable devices operating over the telephone network. The word telefax, short for telefacsimile, for "make a copy at a distance", is also used as a synonym. The device is also known as a telecopier in certain industries.

A "fax machine" usually consists of an image scanner, a modem, and a printer combined into a single package. The scanner converts the content printed on a physical document into a digital image, the modem sends the image data over a phone line to another device, and the printer at the far end produces a copy of the transmitted document.

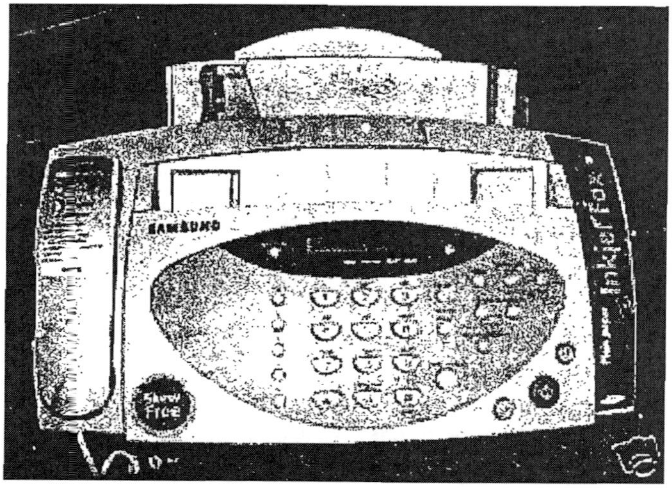

A Samsung fax machine

Some fax machines can be connected to a computer, and the individual components — the scanner, printer, and occasionally the modem — can be used independently. Such devices are usually called multifunction printers or MFPs. Fax capabilities are also offered as options for many high-volume workgroup printers and photocopiers.

Although devices for transmitting printed documents electrically have existed, in various forms, since the mid to late 19th century , modern fax machines became feasible only in the mid-1970s as the sophistication increased and cost of the three underlying technologies dropped. Digital fax machines first became popular in Japan, where they had a clear advantage over competing technologies like the teleprinter, since at the time (before the development of easy-to-use input method editors) it was faster to handwrite kanji than to type the characters. Over time, faxing gradually became affordable, and by the mid-1980s, fax machines were very popular around the world.

Although many businesses still maintain some kind of fax capability, the technology has faced increasing competition from Internet-based systems. However, fax machines still retain some advantages, particularly in the transmission of sensitive material which, due to mandates like Sarbanes-Oxley and HIPAA, cannot be sent over the Internet unencrypted. In the UK, because digital signatures on contracts are not recognized by law, however faxed contracts with a copies of signatures are, and subsequently their continuing popularity in businesses.

In many corporate environments, standalone fax machines have been replaced by "fax servers" and other computerized systems capable of receiving and storing incoming faxes electronically, and then routing them to users on paper or via secure email. Such systems have the advantage of reducing costs by eliminating unnecessary printouts and reducing the number of inbound analog phone lines needed by an office.

Fax Capabilities

There are several different indicators of fax capabilities: Group, class, data transmission rate, and conformance with ITU-T (formerly CCITT) recommendations.

Group

Group 1 and 2 faxes were sent in the same manner as a frame of analog television, with each scanned line transmitted as a continuous analog signal. Horizontal resolution depended upon the quality of the scanner, transmission line, and the printer. Analog fax machines are obsolete and no longer manufactured. ITU-T Recommendations T.2 and T.3 were withdrawn as obsolete in July 1996.

— Group 1 faxes conform to the ITU-T Recommendation T.2. Group 1 faxes take six minutes to transmit a single page, with a vertical resolution of 98 scan lines per inch. Group 1 fax machines are obsolete and no longer manufactured.

— Group 2 faxes conform to the ITU-T Recommendations T.30 and T.3. Group 2 faxes take three minutes to transmit a single page, with a vertical resolution of 100 scan lines per inch. Group 2 fax machines are almost obsolete, and are no longer manufactured. Group 2 fax machines can interoperate with Group 3 fax machines.

Digital : Group 3 and 4 faxes are digital formats, and take advantage of digital compression methods to greatly reduce transmission times.

— Group 3 faxes conform to the ITU-T Recommendations T.30 and T.4. Group 3 faxes take between six and fifteen seconds to transmit a single page (not including the initial time for the fax machines to handshake and synchronize). The horizontal and vertical resolutions are allowed by the T.4 standard to vary among a set of fixed resolutions:

- Horizontal: 100 scan lines per inch
  - vertical: 100 scan lines per inch
- Horizontal: 200 or 204 scan lines per inch
  - Vertical: 100 or 98 scan lines per inch ('Standard')
  - Vertical: 200 or 196 scan lines per inch ('Fine')
  - Vertical: 400 or 391 (note not 392) scan lines per inch ('Superfine')
- Horizontal: 300 scan lines per inch
  - Vertical: 300 scan lines per inch
- Horizontal: 400 or 408 scan lines per inch

— Vertical: 400 or 391 scan lines per inch

— Group 4 faxes conform to the ITU-T Recommendations T.563, T.503, T.521, T.6, T.62, T.70, T.72, T.411 to T.417. They are designed to operate over 64 kbit/s digital ISDN circuits. Their resolution is determined by the T.6 recommendation, which is a superset of the T.4 recommendation.

Fax Over IP (FOIP) Can transmit and receive pre-digitized documents at near realtime speeds. Scanned documents are limited to the amount of time the user takes to load the document in a scanner and for the device to process a digital file. The resolution can vary from as little as 150 DPI to 9600 DPI+. This type of faxing is not like the e-mail to fax service that still uses fax modems at least one way.

Fax class

Computer modems are often designated by a particular fax class, which indicates how much processing is offloaded from the computer's CPU to the fax modem.

— Class 1 fax devices do fax data transfer where the T.4/T.6 data compression and T.30 session management are performed by software on a controlling computer.

— Class 2 fax devices perform T.30 session management themselves, but the T.4/T.6 data compression is performed by software on a controlling computer.

— Class 2.1 fax devices are referred to as "super G3"; they seem to be a little faster than the other 2 classes.

Data transmission rate

Several different telephone line modulation techniques are used by fax machines. They are negotiated during the fax-modem handshake, and the fax devices will use the highest data rate that both fax devices support, usually a minimum of 14.4 kbit/s for Group 3 fax.

ITU Standard	Released Date	Data Rates (bit/s)	Modulation Method
V.27	1988	4800, 2400	PSK
V.29	1988	9600, 7200, 4800	QAM
V.17	1991	14400, 12000, 9600, 7200	TCM
V.34	1994	28800	QAM
V.34bis	1998	33600	QAM

Compression

As well as specifying the resolution (and allowable physical size of the image being faxed), the ITU-T T.4 recommendation specifies two compression methods for decreasing the amount of data that needs to be transmitted between the fax machines to transfer the image. The two methods are:

— Modified Huffman (MH), and

— Modified READ (MR)

Modified Huffman: Modified Huffman (MH) is a codebook-based run-length encoding scheme optimised to efficiently compress whitespace. As most faxes consists mostly of white space, this minimises the transmission time of most faxes. Each line scanned is compressed independently of its predecessor and successor.

Modified Read: Modified Read (MR) encodes the first scanned line using MH. The next line is compared to the first, the differences determined, and then the differences are encoded and transmitted. This is effective as most lines differ little from their predecessor. This is not continued to the end of the fax transmission, but only for a limited number of lines until the process is reset and a new 'first line' encoded with MH is produced. This limited number of lines is to prevent errors propagating throughout the whole fax, as the standard does not provide for error-correction. MR is an optional facility, and some fax machines do not use MR in order to minimise the amount of computation required by the machine. The limited number of lines is two for 'Standard' resolution faxes, and four for 'Fine' resolution faxes.

The ITU-T T.6 recommendation adds a further compression type of Modified READ (MMR), which simply allows for a greater number of lines to be coded by MR than in T.4. This is because T.6 makes the assumption that the transmission is over a circuit with a low number of line errors such as digital ISDN. In this case, there is no maximum number of lines for which the differences are encoded.

Matsushita Whiteline Skip: A proprietary compression scheme employed on Panasonic fax machines is Matsushita Whiteline Skip (MWS). It can be overlaid on the other compression schemes, but is operative only when two Panasonic machines are communicating with one another. This system detects the blank scanned areas between lines of text, and then compresses several blank scan lines into the data space of a single character.

Typical Characteristics

Group 3 fax machines transfer one or a few printed or handwritten pages per minute in black-and-white (bitonal) at a resolution of 100x200 or 200x200 dots per inch. The transfer rate is 14.4 kilobits per second (kbit/s) or higher for modems and some fax machines, but fax machines support speeds beginning with 2400 bit/s and typically operate at 9600 bit/s. The transferred image formats are called ITU-T (formerly CCITT) fax group 3 or 4.

The most basic fax mode transfers black and white only. The original page is scanned in a resolution of 1728 pixels/line and 1145 lines/page (for A4). The resulting raw data is compressed using a modified Huffman code optimized for written text, achieving average compression factors of around 20. Typically a page needs 10 s for transmission, instead of about 3 minutes for the same uncompressed raw data of 1728×1145 bits at a speed of 9600 bit/s. The compression method uses a Huffman codebook for run lengths of black and white runs in a single scanned line, and it can also use the fact that two adjacent scanlines are usually quite similar, saving bandwidth by encoding only the differences.

Fax classes denote the way fax programs interact with fax hardware. Available classes include Class 1, Class 2, Class 2.0 and 2.1, and Intel CAS. Many modems support at least class 1 and often either Class 2 or Class 2.0. Which is preferable to use depends on factors such as hardware, software, modem firmware, and expected use. Fax machines from the 1970s to the 1990s often used direct thermal printers as their printing technology, but since the mid-1990s there has been a transition towards thermal transfer printers, inkjet printers and laser printers.

One of the advantages of inkjet printing is that inkjets can affordably print in colour; therefore, many of the inkjet-based fax machines claim to have colour fax capability. There is a standard called ITU-T30e for faxing in colour; unfortunately, it is not yet widely supported, so many of the colour fax machines can only fax in colour to machines from the same manufacturer.

Alternatives

One popular alternative is to subscribe to an internet fax service. Fax service providers allow users to send and receive faxes from their personal computers using an existing email account. No software, fax server or fax machine is needed. Faxes are received as attached .TIF or .PDF files, or in proprietory formats that require the use of the service provider's software. Faxes can be sent or retrieved from anywhere at any time that a user can get internet access.

Some services even offer secure faxing to comply with stringent HIPAA and Gramm-Leach-Bliley Act requirements to keep Medical Information and Financial Information private and secure. Utilizing a fax service provider is a very popular option because it requires no paper, toner, fax line, etc. and increases efficiency and productivity in the workplace. Being service-based, there are no maintenance, upkeep or licensing issues to manage, keeping faxing as a simple, easy process.

Scottish inventor Alexander Bain is often credited with the first fax patent in 1843. He used his knowledge of electric clock pendulums to produce a back-and-forth line-by-line scanning mechanism. Frederick Bakewell made several improvements on Bain's design and demonstrated the device at the 1851 Great Exhibition in London.

In 1861, the first fax machine, Pantelegraph, was sold by Giovanni Caselli, even before the invention of workable telephones. As a designer for the Radio Corporation of America (RCA), in 1924, Richard H. Ranger invented the wireless photoradiogram, or transoceanic radio facsimile, the forerunner of today's "Fax" machines. A photograph of President Calvin Coolidge sent from New York to London on November 29, 1924 became the first photo picture reproduced by transoceanic radio facsimile. Commercial use of Ranger's product began two years later. Radio fax is still in common use today for transmitting weather charts and information.

An early method for facsimile transmission, the Hellschreiber, was invented in 1929 by Rudolf Hell, a pioneer in mechanical image scanning and transmission.

Prior to the introduction of the now ubiquitous fax machine, one of the first being the Exxon Qwip in the mid-1970s, facsimile machines (the word "fax" had not yet been coined) worked by optical scanning of a document or drawing spinning on a drum. The reflected light, varying in intensity according to the light and dark areas of the document, was focused on a photocell to be converted to an electrical signal varying in frequency. This audio tone was then transmitted using a common telephone handset inserted in an acoustic coupler serving as a modem.

At the receiving end, the same technique (handset in acoustic coupler) converted the varying tone into mechanical movement of a pen or pencil to reproduce the image on a blank sheet of paper on an identical drum rotating at the same rate. A pair of these expensive and bulky machines could only be afforded by companies with a serious need to communicate drawings, design sketches or signed documents between distant locations such as an office and factory.

Fax Server

A fax server is a set of software running on a server computer which is equipped with one or more fax-capable modems attached to telephone lines (or, more recently, software modem emulators which use T.38 ("Fax over IP") technology to transmit the signal over an IP network). Its function is to accept documents from users, convert them into faxes, and transmit them, as well as to receive fax calls and either store the incoming documents or pass them on to users. Users may communicate with the server in several ways, through either a local network or the

Internet. In a big organisation with heavy fax traffic, the computer hosting the fax server may be dedicated to that function, in which case the computer itself may also be known as a fax server.

User Interfaces

For outgoing faxes, several methods are available to the user:

— An e-mail message (with optional attachments) can be sent to a special e-mail address; the fax server monitoring that address converts all such messages into fax format and transmits them.

— The user can tell his computer to "print" a document using a "virtual printer" which, instead of producing a paper printout, sends the document to the fax server, which then transmits it.

— A web interface can be used, allowing files to be uploaded, and transmitted to the fax server for faxing.

— Special client software may be used.

For incoming faxes, several user interfaces may be available:

— The user may be sent an e-mail message for each fax received, with the pages included as attachments, typically in either TIFF or PDF format.

— Incoming faxes may be stored in a dedicated file directory, which the user can monitor.

— A website may allow users to log in and check for received faxes.

— Special client software may be used.

Fax Machines Advantages

Users can send and receive faxes without leaving their desks.

— Any printable computer file can be faxed, without having to first print the document on paper.

— The number of fax lines in an organisation can be reduced, as the server can queue large numbers of faxes and send each when any of a number of lines is free.

— Faxing capability can be added easily to computer programs, allowing automatic generation of faxes.

— Transmitted faxes are more legible and professional-looking.

— There is less clutter of office equipment; incoming faxes can be printed on a standard computer printer.

— Faxing may be monitored and/or recorded, so that users may be allocated quotas or charged fees, or to ensure compliance with data-retention laws.

— Incoming junk faxes are not as much of a problem; the server may maintain a blacklist of numbers it will not accept faxes from (or a white list listing all the numbers it will accept calls from), and those that do get through do not waste paper.

Public Fax Services

There are many companies ("internet fax providers") operating fax servers as a commercial public service. Subscribers can interact with the servers using methods similar to those available for standard fax servers, and would be assigned a dedicated fax number for as long as they maintain their subscription. Fees are normally charged on a flat monthly rate, with a limit on the number of fax pages sent and/or received. Organisations, and individuals in particular, may find this more convenient or cost-effective than operating their own fax systems.

Fax Programmes

An integrated fax programme is a complete set of faxing software which operates on a single computer which is equipped with a fax-capable modem connected to a telephone line. Its user interfaces may be similar to those used to communicate with fax servers, except that since the entire operation takes place on the user's computer the user may be made more aware of the progress of the transmission. Integrated fax programs are aimed at consumers and small organizations, and may sometimes be bundled with the computer's operating system.

COMPUTER AND 3D FAX

3D Fax was an early Windows programme from InfoImaging Technologies. It allowed binary files to be transmitted via fax. Basically, the software encoded the file into a printed image that was sent to the recipient's fax machine. The image was scanned into the receiving computer and 3D Fax decoded it back to its original binary form.

Its functionality was limited. Although being able to send a binary file via fax is a novel idea, it has three main problems:

— First, the size of the binary file is limited to what is possible to encode on a letter-sized piece of paper, so sending anything over 50 kb would require many sheets of paper to print, fax, and scan.

— The second problem is that the sending party requires an adequate printer and a fax machine or fax-modem, and the receiving party requires a scanner and fax (although a fax-modem on both sides would eliminate the printer and scanner requirements). Both also need access to a phone line, to send their fax.

— Finally, most binary files need 100% reliability on the transport. If the binary file is an executable, for example, it needs to be decoded perfectly by the receiving party, or the file simply won't work. This is usually impossible with normal fax transmissions, since they normally have noise and are not 100% copies of the originals. Adding a scan to the process only worsens matters.

The advent of an almost ubiquitous Internet, along with email, made the limited usefulness of this software obsolete.

Error Correction Mode

Error correction mode (ECM) is an optional transmission mode built into Class 1 fax machines or fax modems. ECM automatically detects and corrects errors in the fax transmission process that are sometimes caused by telephone line noise. The page data is divided into what is known as Octets (small blocks of data). Once the receiver has received all the Octets it examines them (using check-sums) and then advises the transmitting fax of any Octets that are in error.

The transmitter then need only resend the blocks in error rather than the whole page. This generally means an ECM coded fax will be more likely to succeed on a noisy line. ECM is the norm rather than the exception. Some fax machines have the capability to enable or disable this function.

FAXLORE

Faxlore is a sort of folklore: an urban legend that is circulated, not by word of mouth, but by fax machine. Xeroxlore is similar material circulated by photocopying. Some faxlore is relatively harmless. Cartoons and jokes often circulate as faxlore; the poor graphic quality becoming worse with each new person who resends the joke to the next recipient. Because faxlore and xeroxlore is the (mis)appropriation of technology owned by the employer, much humorous faxlore is mildly subversive of the workplace and its values.

The somewhat sexist but now semi-traditional lists of reasons "why a cucumber is better than a man" or "why a beer is better than a woman" often circulate as faxlore, as has the well known mock German variations of the "Blinkenlights" poster.

Other sorts of faxlore have had more serious consequences. A number of more notorious urban legends have circulated in faxlore; the notorious "Blue Star Acid" hoax is one well known example; the "lights out" hoax, which claimed that people who were driving in the dark with their headlights out might be gang members, and that those who flashed their headlights at these drivers might be marked for murder as part of a gang initiation, was another hoax that was widely circulated as faxlore. The poor graphic quality of the frequently resent faxes, which often were made out to appear to have originated with the police department of a distant city, only made these hoaxes seem more credible.

In the United States, collections of supposedly sinister symbols have been circulated among school administrators; in the 1980s these symbols were frequently alleged to be "Satanic symbols", and in the 1990s they were alleged to be "gang symbols". Innocuous political or religious symbols, like the peace symbol, the Star of David, the Rosary, the ankh, or the pentagram were mingled with other cryptic or fanciful symbols in these faxed and recirculated sheets, and the entire collection was condemned with the same brush.

On the authority of these anonymous, hard to trace, and impossible to cross-examine sources, school administrators sometimes acted to ban the wearing of Stars of David and similar symbols of minority religions. The incorporation of the symbols of political beliefs and minority religions suggests that at least some instances of this kind of faxlore are deliberate hoaxes with ulterior motives. Sheets of these evil symbols collected by hearsay have occasionally been circulated by local police departments.

Typically, no compiler or author is given for the collection of symbols, though frightening descriptions are often given about their "secret meaning." A number of civil liberties lawsuits were filed over misguided actions taken by school administrators who took these anonymous sources seriously.

A similar claim that the Procter & Gamble logo was a "satanic symbol" was linked in the 1980s to the activity of several Amway distributors, Amway being one of Procter & Gamble's competitors. An occasional hoax with a similar agenda claims that clothing and memorabilia of various universities or sports teams are "gang symbols", for partisan reasons.

With the rise of the Internet, email and the World Wide Web now are available to circulate the sort of material that formerly circulated as faxlore. The hoax warnings of dire and terrible computer viruses that still occasionally circulate, carry on one tradition of the bogus cautionary tale that used to circulate as faxlore. Faxlore, however, is not extinct; the fact that a fax that has been copied several times over, and that the original sender is someone the recipient has never heard of, gives certain kinds of friend of a friend tale additional stature and credibility.

JUNK FAX

Junk faxes are a form of telemarketing where unsolicited advertisements are sent via fax transmission. Junk faxes are the faxed equivalent of spam or junk mail. Proponents of this advertising medium often use the terms broadcast fax or fax advertising to avoid the negative connotation of the term junk fax.

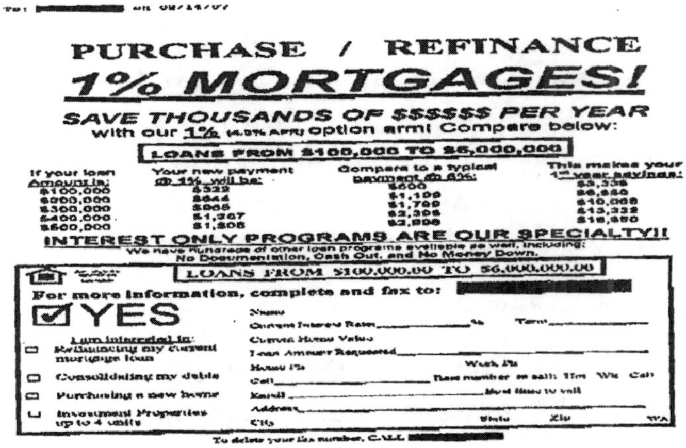

A typical junk fax

Junk faxing came into widespread use in the late 1980s as a result of the development and proliferation of relatively inexpensive desktop fax machines which resulted in rapid growth in the number of fax machines in the U.S. The invention of the computer-based fax board in 1985 by Dr. Hank Magnuski, founder of GammaLink, provided an efficient platform for reaching those fax machines with minimal cost and effort.

The fax machines of this period typically used expensive thermal paper and a common complaint about junk faxes was that they consumed that expensive paper without permission, thus shifting the cost of printing the advertisement to the recipient. Ironically, the U.S. Congress identified one of the most prolific early junk faxers, Mr. Fax of Irvine California, which used junk faxes to advertise the sale of discount fax paper.

In the U.S., the passage of the Telephone Consumer Protection Act in 1991 along with action by individual states reduced the use of junk faxes at that time. However, by the late 1990s junk faxing had once again become a widespread problem in the U.S., with the entry of a number of large-scale fax broadcasters such as fax.com who boasted of the capacity to send millions of fax advertisements per day. Because the legal restrictions of fax advertising are more widely known today, junk faxes are now predominately used in connection with disreputable or fly-by-night marketers.

National Regulations

The Telephone Consumer Protection Act of 1991 (47 USC 227), or TCPA, among other things specifically outlawed junk faxing:

> the use of any telephone facsimile machine, computer, or other device to send an unsolicited advertisement to a telephone facsimile machine (paragraph (b)(1)(C))

The TCPA also requires a fax transmitter to identify the source phone number and transmitting organization or individual on each page. The process of war dialing to determine what phone numbers reach fax machines was also prohibited by the FCC rules under the TCPA.

The TCPA, in particular the junk fax provision, has been challenged in court on First Amendment grounds, but the law has withstood legal challenges.

In 2005, the United States Congress passed the Junk Fax Prevention Act of 2005 which amended the TCPA. The text of the law allows unsolicited fax advertisements if:

> the unsolicited advertisement is from a sender with an established business relationship with the recipient(paragraph (b)(1)(C)(i))

and the sender complies with other requirements.

In April 2006, the Federal Communications Commission (FCC) implemented changes to the fax advertising rules of the TCPA. The new rules:

— codify an established business relationship (EBR) exemption to the prohibition on sending unsolicited fax advertisements;

— define EBR as used in the context of unsolicited fax advertisements;

— require the sender of fax advertisements to provide specified notice and contact information on the fax that allows recipients to "opt-out" of any future transmissions from the sender; and

— specify the circumstances under which a request to "opt-out" complies with the Act. The new rules took effect in August 2006.

In addition to the TCPA, many states also have their own laws regarding junk faxes.

Enforcement

The FCC can investigate violations and impose fines on the violators. Individuals who receive junk faxes can file a complaint with the FCC. Complaints must specify:

— That the sender did not have permission to send the fax (aka unsolicited)

— That the complainant did not have a prior business relationship with the sender

— That the fax was for a good or service

— Any telephone number or addresses included in the fax

— Your name, address, and a telephone number where you can be reached during the day

— The telephone number through which you received the fax advertisement

— A copy of the fax advertisement, if possible, or confirmation that you have retained a copy of the fax

Failure to provide any of the above information may result in the complaint being closed without further action. State authorities can also take actions against violations of the TCPA.

It is also possible for the recipient of a junk fax to bring a private suit against the violator in an appropriate court of their state. Through a private suit, the recipient can either recover the actual monetary loss that resulted from the TCPA violation, or receive $500 in damages for each violation, whichever is greater. The court may triple the damages for each violation if it finds that the defendant acted willingly or knowingly.

TELAUTOGRAPH

The telautograph is an analog precursor to the modern fax machine. Basically it transmits electrical impulses recorded by potentiometers to stepping motors attached to a pen, thus being able to reproduce a drawing or signature made by the sender at the receiver's station. It was the first such device to transmit drawings to a stationary sheet of paper; previous inventions in Europe used rotating drums to make such transmissions.

Its invention is attributed to Elisha Gray, who patented the telautograph in 1888. Descendants of Alexander Graham Bell state that Bell submitted a patent for an earlier version of the telautograph in 1875. Gray's patent stated that the telautograph would allow "one to transmit his own handwriting to a distant point over a two-wire circuit".

Gray was also famous for having submitted his patent application a few hours after Bell had submitted his application for the telephone. The telautograph was first publicly exhibited at the 1893 Chicago World's Columbian Exposition.

As Professor Gray stated in an interview in The Manufacturer & Builder, Vol. 24 No. 4 (1888) at pages 85-6:

> By my invention you can sit down in your office in Chicago, take a pencil in your hand, write a message to me, and as your pencil moves, a pencil here in my laboratory moves simultaneously, and forms the same letters and words in the same way. What you write in Chicago is instantly reproduced here in facsimile. You may write in any language, use a code or cipher, no matter, a facsimile is produced here.
>
> If you want to draw a picture it is the same, the picture is reproduced here. The artist of your newspaper can, by this device, telegraph his pictures of a railway wreck or other occurrences just as a reporter telegraphs his description in words. The artist of your newspaper can, by this device, telegraph his pictures of a railway wreck or other occurrences just as a reporter telegraphs his description in words.

An early telautograph, circa 1880s.

The telautograph became a very popular device for the transmission of signatures over great distances and the device became popular in banks and in large hospitals in order to ensure that doctors orders and patient information was transmitted quickly and accurately throughout the hospital administration.

Telautograph Corporation changed its name several times, in 1971 it was acquired by Arden/Mayfair. In 1993 Danka Industries purchased the company and renamed it Danka/Omnifax. In 1999 Xerox corporation purchased the company and called it the Omnifax division, which has since been absorbed by the corporation.

Transmitting Subscriber Identification (TSID)

The Transmitting Subscriber Identification (TSID) is a string that identifies a fax as a sender. It's sent by a fax machine when sending a fax to a receiving machine. This identification information typically appears in the header area of a received fax and helps recipient to identify the fax machine where the fax originates from. This string is usually a combination of the fax or telephone number and the name of the sender and is often the same as the Called Subscriber Identification (CSID).

10

E-card

An e-card is similar to a postcard or greeting card, with the primary difference being it is created using digital media instead of paper or other traditional materials. E-cards are made available by publishers usually on various Internet sites, where they can be sent to a recipient, usually via e-mail.

E-cards are digital "content", which makes them much more versatile than traditional greeting cards. For example unlike traditional greetings, e-cards can be easily sent to many people at once or extensively personalized by the sender. Conceivably they could be saved to any computer or electronic device or even viewed on a television set, however E-card digital content has not yet progressed as far as digital video or digital audio in terms of varied usage.

Typically an e-card sender chooses from an on-line catalogue of e-cards made available on a publisher's web site. After selecting a card, the sender can personalize it to various degrees by adding a message, photo, or video. Finally the sender specifies the recipient's e-mail address and the web site delivers an e-mail message on behalf of the sender to the recipient.

Printed E-cards

Some e-cards are intended to be printed out rather than sent via e-mail, to most people however are not considered e-cards and are simply home-made greeting cards. The advantage to this over a traditional greeting sometimes can be cost savings, or sometimes simply the ability to "create" something for the recipient rather than choosing a fully completed paper card.

E-card Technology

E-card technology has improved significantly since 1996 around the time of their inception. One technical aspect that has remained mostly constant is the delivery mechanism: The e-mail received by the recipient contains not the e-card itself, but an individually coded link back to the publisher's web site that displays sender's card exactly as it was originally configured.

Use of Postcards

"Postcards" use static (non-moving) images. These were the first type of e-card in use. The recipient sees a single artistic image, accompanied by a personalized greeting message.

Flash Animation

This type of e-card is based on two-dimensional vector animation controlled with a scripting language. The format is proprietary to Adobe, however, widespread usage of Adobe's software allows this type of card to be easily viewed on most of today's computers. The recipient sees an animated short usually 15-30 seconds in duration. The animation often appears to have a cartoon style due to the nature of the content, however, some Flash creations can be quite sophisticated and realistic. A sound track usually accompanies the animation which may contain speech or music.

Flash animated greeting cards can include interactivity, for example, asking the viewer to choose a picture to animate, however, most Flash e-cards are designed to convey the sentiment of the sender through simple observation. Flash animated cards are offered today by almost all major e-card publishers and are consequently the most common format used.

Influence of Mobile Revolution

Traditionally e-cards were sent via computers but with the explosion of mobile phones and its portable technology have given way to e-cards being delivered via mobile phone. Mobile e-cards or 'Mcards' as they are more commonly known were originally created by a UK company called Sharpcards Ltd in 2004. The mcards are purchased via mobile phone networks WAP sites then are downloaded to the mobile then it is sent via MMS straight the recipients handset.

Importance of E-Card

The greeting card metaphor was employed early in the life of the World Wide Web, and by Valentine's Day 1996 it was popular enough to be documented. That year, Valentine's cards were offered by Infobahn.com and Sony Entertainment, among others.

In October 1999, Excite@Home bought the web site Blue Mountain Arts for $780M . The transaction has been referenced by CNN and Business 2.0 as evidence of the Dot-com bubble. On September 13, 2001, three weeks before filing for bankruptcy on October 1, 2001, Excite@Home sold BlueMountain.com to American Greetings for $35M, or $3.23 per unique monthly user. The web site BlueMountain.com remains a large web site, primarily focused on E-Cards. In May 2007 MushyGushy.com became the first E-Card site to allow users to personalize E-Greetings based on ethnicity, skin-tone, and gender.

Originally, most E-Cards were free, by virtue of being sponsored by advertising. While free greeting cards are still the most prevalent and popular, some sites charge for either all e-cards or special premium e-cards.

Since many e-card companies are privy to the e-mail address of the recipient and often also the sender, and whether the recipient reads the card, spammers can use E-Cards for finding active e-mail addresses.

Sending an e-card to a given recipient invariably involves giving that recipient's email address to the e-card service — a third party. As with other third-party email services (such as mailing-list companies), the operator has the chance to misuse this address. One example of misuse is if the e-card service sends advertisements to the recipient's address. Under anti-spam rules used by major ISPs, such advertisements would be spam, since the recipient never asked ("opted in") to receive them. The e-card sender as well as the service could be held responsible for the act of spamming, since while the service sent the spam, the e-card sender provided the address.

In some cases, it may be illegal for an organization or business to use an e-card service to send greetings to its customers. For instance, data privacy laws may forbid a business from disclosing information about customers to a third party — including names and email addresses.

In late June 2007 a spat of emails with the subject line "You've received a postcard from a family member!" and other similar subjects, was seen making their way across the internet. Unfortunately most of these emails contained links to malicious web sites where javascript was used to exploit the browser in order to compromise a system.

Cardmaking Method

Cardmaking is the craft of handmaking greeting cards. Many people with interests in allied crafts such as scrapbooking and stamping have begun to use their skills to start making handmade cards. This has contributed to cardmaking becoming a popular hobby.

Publishers have also been quick to cash in on the popularity of cardmaking, with several monthly magazines in the US and UK devoted to the topic. There have also been over 150 books on handmade cards published . Traditional high street stores have begun to devote an increasing amount of their floorspace to handmade cards. Handmade products are now being seen by retailers as a way to increase margins, and handmade cards are no exception. This is particularly the case as mass produced printed greeting cards have been faced with competition from electronic greeting cards. Over seven billion greeting cards were sent in the US alone last year; greeting cards are a multi-billion dollar business.

In contrast, hundreds of small businesses have been setup by avid crafters keen to make a return on their cardmaking efforts. Many of these are taking advantages of the low setup costs of web-based selling and the wide customer-base of auction sites like eBay. Many others continue to sell their creations at craft fairs, markets and fêtes. Others use their cardmaking skills to turn a profit in the wedding planning market making handmade wedding invitations and favours.

The custom of sending greeting cards can be traced back to the ancient Chinese, who exchanged messages of good will to celebrate the New Year, and to the early Egyptians, who conveyed their greetings on papyrus scrolls. By the early 1400s, handmade paper greeting cards were being exchanged in Europe. The Germans are known to have printed New Year's greetings from woodcuts as early as 1400, and handmade paper Valentines were being exchanged in various parts of Europe in the early to mid-1400s.

However, by the 1850s, the greeting card had been transformed from a relatively expensive, handmade and hand-delivered gift to a popular and affordable means of personal communication, due largely to advances in printing and mechanization.

This trend continued, followed by new trends like Christmas cards, the first of which appeared in published form in London in 1843 when Sir Henry Cole hired artist John Calcott Horsley to design a holiday card that he could send to his friends and acquaintances. Technical developments like colour lithography in 1930 propelled the manufactured greeting card industry forward.

During the 1980s the trend began to turn, with consumers increasing looking for greeting cards that were differentiated from the standard offering. In the late 1990s the market was clearly beginning to separate in to three different segments:

— handmade and premium cards

— mass-manufactured cards

— e-cards

11
E-mail Spoofing

E-mail spoofing is a term used to describe fraudulent email activity in which the sender address and other parts of the email header are altered to appear as though the email originated from a different source. E-mail spoofing is a technique commonly used for spam e-mail and phishing to hide the origin of an e-mail message. By changing certain properties of the e-mail, such as the From, Return-Path and Reply-To fields (which can be found in the message header), ill-intentioned users can make the e-mail appear to be from someone other than the actual sender. It is often associated with website spoofing which mimic an actual, well-known website but are run by another party either with fraudulent intentions or as a means of criticism of the organization's activities.

E-mail Spoofing Methods

As many spammers now use special software to create random sender addresses, even if the user finds the origin of the e-mail it is unlikely that the e-mail address will be active.

The technique is now used ubiquitously by mass-mailing worms as a means of concealing the origin of the propagation. On infection, worms such as ILOVEYOU,

Klez and Sober will often try to perform searches for e-mail addresses within the address book of a mail client, and use those addresses in the From field of e-mails that they send, so that these e-mails appear to have been sent by the third party. For example:

> User1 is sent an infected e-mail and then the e-mail is opened, triggering propagation. The worm finds the addresses of User2 and User3 within the address book of User1. From the computer of User1, the worm sends an infected e-mail to User2, but the e-mail appears to have been sent from User3

This can be particularly problematic in a corporate setting, where e-mail is sent to organisations with content filtering gateways in place. These gateways are often configured with default rules that send reply notices for messages that get blocked, so the example is often followed by:

> User2 doesn't receive the message, but instead gets a message telling him that a virus sent to them has been blocked. User3 receives a message telling him that a virus sent by them has been blocked. This creates confusion for both User2 and User3, while User1 remains unaware of the actual infection.

Computer Virus

A computer virus is a computer programme that can copy itself and infect a computer without permission or knowledge of the user. The original may modify the copies or the copies may modify themselves, as occurs in a metamorphic virus. A virus can only spread from one computer to another when its host is taken to the uninfected computer, for instance by a user sending it over a network or carrying it on a removable medium such as a floppy disk, CD, USB drive or by the Internet. Additionally, viruses can spread to other computers by infecting files on a network file system or a file system that is accessed by another computer. Viruses are sometimes confused with computer worms and Trojan horses. A worm can spread itself to other computers without needing to be transferred as part of a host, and a Trojan horse is a file that appears harmless until executed.

Many personal computers are now connected to the Internet and to local area networks, facilitating the spread of malicious code. Today's viruses may also take advantage of network services such as the World Wide Web, e-mail, and file sharing systems to spread, blurring the line between viruses and worms. Furthermore, some sources use an alternative terminology in which a virus is any form of self-replicating malware.

Some viruses are programmed to damage the computer by damaging programs, deleting files, or reformatting the hard disk. Others are not designed to do any damage, but simply replicate themselves and perhaps make their presence known by presenting text, video, or audio messages. Even these benign viruses can create problems for the computer user. They typically take up computer memory used by legitimate programs. As a result, they often cause erratic behaviour and can result in system crashes. In addition, many viruses are bug-ridden, and these bugs may lead to system crashes and data loss.

The Creeper virus was first detected on Arpanet, the forerunner of the Internet in the early 1970s. It propagated via the Tanex operating system and could make use of any connect modem to dial out to remote computers and infect them. It would display the message "I'm The Creeper : Catch me if you can.". It is rumored that the Reaper programme that appeared shortly after and sought out copies of the Creeper and deleted them, may have been written by the creator of the Creeper in a fit of regret.

A programme called "Elk Cloner" is commonly credited with being the first computer virus to appear "in the wild" - that is, outside the single computer or lab where it was created, but that claim is false. The Timeline of notable computer viruses and worms for other earlier viruses. It was however the first virus to infect computers "in the home". Written in 1982 by Richard Skrenta, it attached itself to the Apple DOS 3.3 operating system and spread by floppy disk. This virus was originally a joke, created by a high school student and put onto a game.

The disk could only be used 49 times. The game was set to play, but release the virus on the 50th time of starting the game. Only this time, instead of playing the game, it would change to a blank screen that read a poem about the virus named Elk Cloner. The poem that showed up on the screen is as follows: It will get on all your disks. It will infiltrate your chips. Yes it's Cloner! It will stick to you like glue. It will modify RAM too. Send in the Cloner! The computer would then be infected.

The first PC virus was a boot sector virus called (c)Brain, created in 1986 by two brothers, Basit and Amjad Farooq Alvi, operating out of Lahore, Pakistan. The brothers reportedly created the virus to deter pirated copies of software they had written. However, analysts have claimed that the Ashar virus, a variant of Brain, possibly predated it based on code within the virus.

Before computer networks became widespread, most viruses spread on removable media, particularly floppy disks. In the early days of the personal computer, many users regularly exchanged information and programs on floppies. Some viruses spread by infecting programs stored on these disks, while others installed themselves into the disk boot sector, ensuring that they would be run when the user booted the computer from the disk.

Traditional computer viruses emerged in the 1980s, driven by the spread of personal computers and the resultant increase in BBS and modem use, and software sharing. Bulletin board driven software sharing contributed directly to the spread of Trojan horse programs, and viruses were written to infect popularly traded software. Shareware and bootleg software were equally common vectors for viruses on BBS's. Within the "pirate scene" of hobbyists trading illicit copies of retail software, traders in a hurry to obtain the latest applications and games were easy targets for viruses.

Since the mid-1990s, macro viruses have become common. Most of these viruses are written in the scripting languages for Microsoft programs such as Word and Excel. These viruses spread in Microsoft Office by infecting documents and spreadsheets. Since Word and Excel were also available for Mac OS, most of these viruses were able to spread on Macintosh computers as well. Most of these viruses did not have the ability to send infected e-mail. Those viruses which did spread through e-mail took advantage of the Microsoft Outlook COM interface.

Macro viruses pose unique problems for detection software. For example, some versions of Microsoft Word allowed macros to replicate themselves with additional blank lines. The virus behaved identically but would be misidentified as a new virus. In another example, if two macro viruses simultaneously infect a document, the combination of the two, if also self-replicating, can appear as a "mating" of the two and would likely be detected as a virus unique from the "parents".

A virus may also send a web address link as an instant message to all the contacts on an infected machine. If the recipient, thinking the link is from a friend (a trusted source) follows the link to the website, the virus hosted at the site may be able to infect this new computer and continue propagating.

The newest species of the virus family is the cross-site scripting virus. The virus emerged from research and was academically demonstrated in 2005 . This virus utilizes cross-site scripting vulnerabilities to propagate. Since 2005 there have been multiple instances of the cross-site scripting viruses in the wild, most notable sites affected have been MySpace and Yahoo.

Etymology

The word virus is derived from and used in the same sense as the biological equivalent. The term "virus" is often used in common parlance to describe all kinds of malware (malicious software), including those that are more properly classified as worms or Trojans. Most popular antivirus software packages defend against all of these types of attack. In some technical communities, the term "virus" is also extended to include the authors of malware, in an insulting sense. The English plural of "virus" is "viruses". Some people use "virii" or "viri" as a plural, but this is rare. For a discussion about whether "viri" and "virii" are correct alternatives of "viruses".

The first known use of the term virus related to computers is in a 1972 science fiction novel by David Gerrold, When H.A.R.L.I.E. Was One,. The book describes a fictional computer programme called "VIRUS" that worked just like a virus (and was countered by a programme called "VACCINE"). The term "computer virus" with current usage appears in the comic book Uncanny X-Men #158, written by Chris Claremont and published in 1982.

The 1973 movie "Westworld" doesn't actually use the word virus, but a scientist refers to "an analogy to an infectious disease process spreading" to explain endemic robot malfunctions. Another scientist from the film adds that it's "It's only a theoretical concept." The first academic use of the term was first used in a publication by Fred Cohen in his 1984 paper Experiments with Computer Viruses, where he credits Len Adleman with coining it.

Replication Strategies

In order to replicate itself, a virus must be permitted to execute code and write to memory. For this reason, many viruses attach themselves to executable files that may be part of legitimate programs. If a user tries to start an infected programme, the virus' code may be executed first. Viruses can be divided into two types, on the basis of their behaviour when they are executed. Nonresident viruses immediately search for other hosts that can be infected, infect these targets, and finally transfer control to the application programme they infected. Resident viruses do not search for hosts when they are started. Instead, a resident virus loads itself into memory on execution and transfers control to the host programme. The virus stays active in the background and infects new hosts when those files are accessed by other programs or the operating system itself.

Nonresident viruses can be thought of as consisting of a finder module and a replication module. The finder module is responsible for finding new files to infect. For each new executable file the finder module encounters, it calls the replication module to infect that file.

Resident viruses contain a replication module that is similar to the one that is employed by nonresident viruses. However, this module is not called by a finder module. Instead, the virus loads the replication module into memory when it is executed and ensures that this module is executed each time the operating system is called to perform a certain operation. For example, the replication module can be called each time the operating system executes a file. In this case, the virus infects every suitable programme that is executed on the computer.

Resident viruses are sometimes subdivided into a category of fast infectors and a category of slow infectors. Fast infectors are designed to infect as many files as possible. For instance, a fast infector can infect every potential host file that is accessed. This poses a special problem to antivirus software, since a virus scanner will access every potential host file on a computer when it performs a system-wide scan. If the virus scanner fails to notice that such a virus is present in memory, the virus can "piggy-back" on the virus scanner and in this way infect all files that are scanned. Fast infectors rely on their fast infection rate to spread.

The disadvantage of this method is that infecting many files may make detection more likely, because the virus may slow down a computer or perform many suspicious actions that can be noticed by antivirus software. Slow infectors, on the other hand, are designed to infect hosts infrequently. For instance, some slow infectors only infect files when they are copied. Slow infectors are designed to avoid detection by limiting their actions: they are less likely to slow down a computer noticeably, and will at most infrequently trigger antivirus software that detects suspicious behaviour by programs. The slow infector approach does not seem very successful, however.

Vectors and Hosts

Viruses have targeted various types of transmission media or hosts. This list is not exhaustive:

- — Binary executable files (such as COM files and EXE files in MS-DOS, Portable Executable files in Microsoft Windows, and ELF files in Linux)
- — Volume Boot Records of floppy disks and hard disk partitions
- — The master boot record (MBR) of a hard disk
- — General-purpose script files (such as batch files in MS-DOS and Microsoft Windows, VBScript files, and shell script files on Unix-like platforms).
- — Application-specific script files (such as Telix-scripts)
- — Documents that can contain macros (such as Microsoft Word documents, Microsoft Excel spreadsheets, AmiPro documents, and Microsoft Access database files)
- — Cross-site scripting vulnerabilities in web applications

Inhospitable vectors

It is difficult, but not impossible, for viruses to tag along in source files, seeing that computer languages are built for human eyes and experienced operators. With the notable exception of WMF, it is almost impossible for viruses to tag along in data files like MP3s, MPGs, OGGs, JPGs, GIFs, PNGs, MNGs, PDFs, and DVI files (this is not an exhaustive list of generally trusted file types). Even if a virus were to 'infect' such a file, it would be inoperative since there would be no way for the viral code to be executed.

A caveat must be mentioned from PDFs, that like HTML, may link to malicious code. Further, an exploitable buffer overflow in a programme which reads the data files could be used to trigger the execution of code hidden within the data file, but this attack is substantially mitigated in computer architectures with an execute disable bit.

It is worth noting that some virus authors have written an .EXE extension on the end of .PNG (for example), hoping that users would stop at the trusted file type without noticing that the computer would start with the final type of file.

Avoid Detection

In order to avoid detection by users, some viruses employ different kinds of deception. Some old viruses, especially on the MS-DOS platform, make sure that the "last modified" date of a host file stays the same when the file is infected by the virus. This approach does not fool antivirus software, however, especially that which maintains and dates Cyclic Redundancy Codes on file changes.

Some viruses can infect files without increasing their sizes or damaging the files. They accomplish this by overwriting unused areas of executable files. These are called cavity viruses. For example the CIH virus, or Chernobyl Virus, infects Portable Executable files. Because those files had many empty gaps, the virus, which was 1 KB in length, did not add to the size of the file.

Some viruses try to avoid detection by killing the tasks associated with antivirus software before it can detect them. As computers and operating systems grow larger and more complex, old hiding techniques need to be updated or replaced. Defending your computer against viruses may demand that your file system migrate towards detailed and explicit permission for every kind of file access.

A virus needs to infect hosts in order to spread further. In some cases, it might be a bad idea to infect a host programme. For example, many antivirus programs perform an integrity check of their own code. Infecting such programs will therefore increase the likelihood that the virus is detected. For this reason, some viruses are programmed not to infect programs that are known to be part of antivirus software. Another type of host that viruses sometimes avoid is bait files. Bait files (or goat files) are files that are specially created by antivirus software, or by antivirus professionals themselves, to be infected by a virus. These files can be created for various reasons, all of which are related to the detection of the virus:

— Antivirus professionals can use bait files to take a sample of a virus (i.e. a copy of a programme file that is infected by the virus). It is more practical to store and exchange a small, infected bait file, than to exchange a large application programme that has been infected by the virus.

— Antivirus professionals can use bait files to study the behaviour of a virus and evaluate detection methods. This is especially useful when the virus is polymorphic. In this case, the virus can be made to infect a large number of bait files. The infected files can be used to test whether a virus scanner detects all versions of the virus.

— Some antivirus software employs bait files that are accessed regularly. When these files are modified, the antivirus software warns the user that a virus is probably active on the system.

Since bait files are used to detect the virus, or to make detection possible, a virus can benefit from not infecting them. Viruses typically do this by avoiding suspicious programs, such as small programme files or programs that contain certain patterns of 'garbage instructions'.

A related strategy to make baiting difficult is sparse infection. Sometimes, sparse infectors do not infect a host file that would be a suitable candidate for infection in other circumstances. For example, a virus can decide on a random basis whether to infect a file or not, or a virus can only infect host files on particular days of the week.

Some viruses try to trick antivirus software by intercepting its requests to the operating system. A virus can hide itself by intercepting the antivirus software's request to read the file and passing the request to the virus, instead of the OS. The virus can then return an uninfected version of the file to the antivirus software, so that it seems that the file is "clean". Modern antivirus software employs various techniques to counter stealth mechanisms of viruses. The only completely reliable method to avoid stealth is to boot from a medium that is known to be clean.

Most modern antivirus programs try to find virus-patterns inside ordinary programs by scanning them for so-called virus signatures. A signature is a characteristic byte-pattern that is part of a certain virus or family of viruses. If a virus scanner finds such a pattern in a file, it notifies the user that the file is infected. The user can then delete, or (in some cases) "clean" or "heal" the infected file. Some viruses employ techniques that make detection by means of signatures difficult but probably not impossible. These viruses modify their code on each infection. That is, each infected file contains a different variant of the virus.

Encryption with a variable key: A more advanced method is the use of simple encryption to encipher the virus. In this case, the virus consists of a small decrypting module and an encrypted copy of the virus code. If the virus is encrypted with a different key for each infected file, the only part of the virus that remains constant is the decrypting module, which would (for example) be appended to the end. In this case, a virus scanner cannot directly detect the virus using signatures, but it can still detect the decrypting module, which still makes indirect detection of the virus possible. Since these would be symmetric keys, stored on the infected host, it is in fact entirely possible to decrypt the final virus, but that probably isn't required, since self-modifying code is such a rarity that it may be reason for virus scanners to at least flag the file as suspicious.

An old, but compact, encryption involves XORing each byte in a virus with a constant, so that the exclusive-or operation had only to be repeated for decryption. It is suspicious code that modifies itself, so the code to do the encryption/decryption may be part of the signature in many virus definitions.

Polymorphic code: Polymorphic code was the first technique that posed a serious threat to virus scanners. Just like regular encrypted viruses, a polymorphic virus infects files with an encrypted copy of itself, which is decoded by a decryption module. In the case of polymorphic viruses however, this decryption module is also modified on each infection. A well-written polymorphic virus therefore has no parts that stay the same on each infection, making it very difficult to detect directly using signatures. Antivirus software can detect it by decrypting the viruses using an emulator, or by statistical pattern analysis of the encrypted virus body. To enable polymorphic code, the virus has to have a polymorphic engine (also called mutating engine or mutation engine) somewhere in its encrypted body.

Some viruses employ polymorphic code in a way that constrains the mutation rate of the virus significantly. For example, a virus can be programmed to mutate only slightly over time, or it can be programmed to refrain from mutating when it infects a file on a computer that already contains copies of the virus.

The advantage of using such slow polymorphic code is that it makes it more difficult for antivirus professionals to obtain representative samples of the virus, because bait files that are infected in one run will typically contain identical or similar samples of the virus. This will make it more likely that the detection by the virus scanner will be unreliable, and that some instances of the virus may be able to avoid detection.

Metamorphic code: To avoid being detected by emulation, some viruses rewrite themselves completely each time they are to infect new executables. Viruses that use this technique are said to be metamorphic. To enable metamorphism, a metamorphic engine is needed. A metamorphic virus is usually very large and complex. For example, W32/Simile consisted of over 14000 lines of Assembly language code, 90% of it part of the metamorphic engine.

Vulnerability and Countermeasures

Operating systems to viruses

Just as genetic diversity in a population decreases the chance of a single disease wiping out a population, the diversity of software systems on a network similarly limits the destructive potential of viruses.

This became a particular concern in the 1990s, when Microsoft gained market dominance in desktop operating systems and office suites. The users of Microsoft software (especially networking software such as Microsoft Outlook and Internet Explorer) are especially vulnerable to the spread of viruses. Microsoft software is targeted by virus writers due to their desktop dominance, and is often criticized for including many errors and holes for virus writers to exploit. Integrated applications (such as Microsoft Office) and applications with scripting languages with access to the file system (for example Visual Basic Script (VBS), and applications with networking features) are also particularly vulnerable.

Although Windows is by far the most popular operating system for virus writers, some viruses also exist on other platforms. Any operating system that allows third-party programs to run can theoretically run viruses. Some operating systems are less secure than others. Unix-based OS's (and NTFS-aware applications on Windows NT based platforms) only allow their users to run executables within their protected space in their own directories.

As of 2006, there are relatively few security exploits targeting Mac OS X (with a Unix-based file system); the known vulnerabilities fall under the classifications of worms and Trojans. The number of viruses for the older Apple operating systems, known as Mac OS Classic, varies greatly from source to source, with Apple stating that there are only four known viruses, and independent sources stating there are as many as 63 viruses. It is safe to say that Macs are less likely to be exploited due to their secure Unix base, and because a Mac-specific virus could only infect a small proportion of computers (making the effort less desirable). Virus vulnerability between Macs and Windows is a chief selling point, one that Apple uses in their Get a Mac advertising.

Windows and Unix have similar scripting abilities, but while Unix natively blocks normal users from having access to make changes to the operating system environment, Windows does not. In 1997, when a virus for Linux was released - known as "Bliss" - leading antivirus vendors issued warnings that Unix-like systems could fall prey to viruses just like Windows.

The Bliss virus may be considered characteristic of viruses - as opposed to worms - on Unix systems. Bliss requires that the user run it explicitly (making it a trojan), and it can only infect programs that the user has the access to modify. Unlike Windows users, most Unix users do not log in as an administrator user except to install or configure software; as a result, even if a user ran the virus, it could not harm their operating system. The Bliss virus never became widespread, and remains chiefly a research curiosity.

Software development

Because software is often designed with security features to prevent unauthorized use of system resources, many viruses must exploit software bugs in a system or application to spread. Software development strategies that produce large numbers of bugs will generally also produce potential exploits.

Other preventive countermeasures

Many users install antivirus software that can detect and eliminate known viruses after the computer downloads or runs the executable. There are two common methods that an antivirus software application uses to detect viruses. The first, and by far the most common method of virus detection is using a list of virus signature definitions. This works by examining the content of the computer's memory (its RAM, and boot sectors) and the files stored on fixed or removable drives (hard drives, floppy drives), and comparing those files against a database of known virus "signatures".

The disadvantage of this detection method is that users are only protected from viruses that pre-date their last virus definition update. The second method is to use a heuristic algorithm to find viruses based on common behaviors. This method has the ability to detect viruses that antivirus security firms' have yet to create a signature for.

Some antivirus programs are able to scan opened files in addition to sent and received emails 'on the fly' in a similar manner. This practice is known as "on-access scanning." Antivirus software does not change the underlying capability of host software to transmit viruses. Users must update their software regularly to patch security holes. Antivirus software also needs to be regularly updated in order to prevent the latest threats.

One may also prevent the damage done by viruses by making regular backups of data (and the Operating Systems) on different media, that are either kept unconnected to the system (most of the time), read-only or not accessible for other reasons, such as using different file systems. This way, if data is lost through a virus, one can start again using the backup (which should preferably be recent). If a backup session on optical media like CD and DVD is closed, it becomes read-only and can no longer be affected by a virus. Likewise, an Operating System on a bootable can be used to start the computer if the installed Operating Systems become unusable.

Another method is to use different Operating Systems on different file systems. A virus is not likely to affect both. Data backups can also be put on different file systems. For example, Linux requires specific software to write to NTFS partitions, so if one does not install such software and uses a separate installation of MS Windows to make the backups on an NTFS partition (and preferably only for that reason), the backup should remain safe from any Linux viruses. Likewise, MS Windows can not read file systems like ext3, so if one normally uses MS Windows, the backups can be made on an ext3 partition using a Linux installation.

Once a computer has been compromised by a virus, it is usually unsafe to continue using the same computer without completely reinstalling the operating system. However, there are a number of recovery options that exist after a computer has a virus. These actions depend on severity of the type of virus.

Virus removal: One possibility on Windows XP is a tool known as System Restore, which restores the registry and critical system files to a previous checkpoint. Often a virus will cause a system to hang, and a subsequent hard reboot will render a system restore point from the same day corrupt. Restore points from previous days should work provided the virus is not designed to corrupt the restore files. Some viruses, however, disable system restore and other important tools such as Task Manager and Command Prompt. An examples virus that does this is CiaDoor.

Administrators have the option to disable such tools from limited users for various reasons. The virus modifies the registry to do the same, except, when the Administrator is controlling the computer, it blocks all users from accessing the tools. When an infected tool activates it gives the message "Task Manager has been disabled by your administrator.", even if the user trying to open the programme is the administrator.

Operating system reinstallation: As a last ditch effort, if a virus is on your system and anti-viral software can't clean it, then reinstalling the operating system may be required. To do this properly, the hard drive is completely erased (partition deleted and formatted) and the operating system is e, and separately scanned for infection before erasing the original hard drive and reinstalling installed from media known not to be infected. Important files should first be backed up, if possible.

Computer Worm

A computer worm is a self-replicating computer programme. It uses a network to send copies of itself to other nodes (computer terminals on the network) and it may do so without any user intervention. Unlike a virus, it does not need to attach itself to an existing programme. Worms always harm the network (if only by consuming bandwidth), whereas viruses always infect or corrupt files on a targeted computer.

Naming and History

The name worm comes from The Shockwave Rider, a science fiction novel published in 1975 by John Brunner. Researchers John F Shoch and Jon A Hupp of Xerox PARC chose the name in a paper published in 1982; The Worm Programs, Comm ACM, 25(3):172-180, 1982), and it has since been widely adopted.

The first implementation of a worm was by these same two researchers at Xerox PARC in 1978. Shoch and Hupp originally designed the worm to find idle processors on the network and assign them tasks, sharing the processing load, and so improving the 'CPU cycle use efficiency' across an entire network. They were self-limited so that they would spread no farther than intended.

Payload for Worms

Many worms have been created which are only designed to spread, and don't attempt to alter the systems they pass through. However, as the Morris worm and Mydoom showed, the network traffic and other unintended effects can often cause major disruption. A payload is code designed to do more than spread the worm - it might delete files on a host system (e.g., the ExploreZip worm), encrypt files in a cryptoviral extortion attack, or send documents via e-mail.

A very common payload for worms is to install a backdoor in the infected computer to allow the creation of a "zombie" under control of the worm author - Sobig and Mydoom are examples which created zombies. Networks of such machines are often referred to as botnets and are very commonly used by spam senders for sending junk email or to cloak their website's address. Spammers are therefore thought to be a source of funding for the creation of such worms, and worm writers have been caught selling lists of IP addresses of infected machines. Others try to blackmail companies with threatened DoS attacks.

Backdoors, however they may be installed, can be exploited by other malware, including worms. Examples include Doomjuice, which spreads using the backdoor opened by Mydoom, and at least one instance of malware taking advantage of the rootkit backdoor installed by the Sony/BMG DRM software utilized by millions of music CDs prior to late 2005.

Worms with Good Intent

Beginning with the very first research into worms at Xerox PARC there have been attempts to create useful worms. The Nachi family of worms, for example, tried to download and install patches from Microsoft's website to fix vulnerabilities in the host system - by exploiting those same vulnerabilities. In practice, although this may have made these systems more secure, it generated considerable network traffic, rebooted the machine in the course of patching it, and, most importantly, did its work without the consent of the computer's owner or user. Most security experts regard all worms as malware, whatever their payload or their writers' intentions.

Dangerous Computer Worms

Worms spread by exploiting vulnerabilities in operating systems. If user interaction is required to for the malware to spread, it is called a trojan horse. All vendors supply regular security updates, and if these are installed to a machine then the majority of worms are unable to spread to it. If a vendor acknowledges a vulnerability but has yet to release a security update to patch it, a zero day exploit is possible. However, these are relatively rare.

Users need to be wary of opening unexpected email, and should not run attached files or programs, or visit web sites that are linked to such emails. However, as the I LoveYou worm showed, and as phishing attacks become more efficient, tricking users will always be possible. Antivirus and anti-spyware software are helpful, but must be kept up-to-date with new pattern files at least every few days. The use of a firewall is also recommemded.

Hoaxes

A hoax is an attempt to trick an audience into believing that something false is real. There is often some material object (e.g., snake oil) involved which is actually a forgery; however, it is possible to perpetrate a hoax by making only true statements using unfamiliar wording or context. Unlike a fraud or con (which is usually aimed at a single victim and are made for illicit financial or material gain), a hoax is often perpetrated as a practical joke, to cause embarrassment, or to provoke social change by making people aware of something.

Many hoaxes are motivated by a desire to satirize or educate by exposing the credulity of the public and the media or the absurdity of the target. For instance, the hoaxes of James Randi poke fun at believers in the paranormal. The many hoaxes of Alan Abel and Joey Skaggs satirize people's willingness to believe the media. Political hoaxes are sometimes motivated by the desire to ridicule or besmirch opposing politicians or political institutions, often before elections.

Governments often perpetrate hoaxes to assist them with unpopular aims such as going to war (e.g., the Ems Telegram). In fact, there is often a mixture of outright hoax, and suppression and management of information to give the desired impression. In wartime, rumours abound; some may be deliberate hoaxes.

There is often considerable controversy about whether a given factoid is true or a hoax. The word hoax is said to have come from the common magic incantation hocus pocus. "Hocus pocus", in turn, is commonly believed to be a distortion of "hoc est corpus" ("this is the body") from the Latin Mass. Many etymologists dispute the latter claim.

Hoaxes Character

Hoaxes are not always created, initiated or sourced the same way. Examples:

- — Hoax by tradition
- — Hoax by design
- — Hoax originating in legitimate non-hoax use
- — Hoax by scare tactics
- — Urban legend

This is by no means a complete list; but the import is to show that hoaxes take many forms. The main characteristic of hoaxes is presenting the information or media as something real or believable to human understanding but is in fact false. Whether there is intent to deceive is not part of the hoax characteristics, as hoaxes are known both with and without it.

Other Hoaxes

— Orson Welles' Mercury Theatre radio broadcast on October 30, 1938, entitled "The War of the Worlds" has been called the "single greatest media hoax of all time", although it was not - Welles said - intended to be a hoax. The broadcast was heard on CBS radio stations throughout the United States. Despite repeated announcements within the programme that it was a work of fiction, many listeners tuning in during the programme believed that the world was being attacked by invaders from Mars. Rebroadcasts in South America also had this effect even to a greater extent. It has also been suggested that the story of the hoax is, in fact, a hoax, or at least a significant exaggeration: that the broadcast did not cause widespread panic .

— Wolfgang von Kempelen's construction of the chess-playing Mechanical Turk in 1770.

— The Protocols of the Elders of Zion is an antisemitic literary forgery that purports to describe a Jewish plot to achieve world domination.

— The 1934 "Surgeon's Photograph" of the Loch Ness monster, revealed some sixty years later to have been a plastic head and neck mounted to a toy submarine.

— The Bathtub hoax, perpetrated by American journalist and satirist H. L. Mencken in 1918, which was cited as factual even after the hoax had been revealed by the author.

— The Great Moon Hoax of 1835, which helped to establish the market position of the New York Sun.

— The Cardiff Giant of 1869, which was created and "discovered"; reputedly after an argument about the reality of giants.

— Our First Time, possibly one of the first major internet hoaxes, although some characterized it as a botched scam.

— Idaho, the northwestern US state, was named as the result of a hoax. Lobbyist George M. Willing suggested the name, claiming it was a Native American term meaning "gem of the mountains." It was later discovered that Willing had made up the word himself. As a result, the original Idaho Territory was renamed Colorado. Eventually, the controversy was forgotten and the made-up name stuck.

— The Sokal hoax was a fake paper published in the journal Social Text, which was intended to reveal the uncritical misuse of scientific terms and ignorance of science in the field of postmodern cultural studies.

— The Piltdown Man fraud caused some embarrassment to the field of paleontology when apparently ancient hominid remains discovered in England in 1912 were revealed as a hoax some 41 years later.

— In 1970, Clifford Irving and Richard Suskind contrived to write an autobiography of Howard Hughes, believing Hughes would not come out of hiding to denounce it. Irving sent a manuscript to his publisher McGraw-Hill in late 1971. Authentication tests and Hughes's initial silence led some to believe the manuscript was genuine, but Hughes eventually gave a teleconference by phone denying both participation in the book and knowledge of Irving. Weeks later, Irving confessed to the hoax and was later convicted of fraud. He served 17 months of a two and a half year prison sentence. Suskind, sentenced to six months, served five.

— The Hitler Diaries; the 1983 forgeries claiming to be the diaries of Adolf Hitler.

— In 1928 Margaret Mead published Coming of Age in Samoa, a book largely concerned with the sexual practices of adolescents in Samoa. In 1983, five years after Mead's death, Derek Freeman published Margaret Mead and Samoa: The Making and Unmaking of an Anthropological Myth, in which he said that he had interviewed the sources of Mead's information, and was told that they had hoaxed Mead. Freeman's conclusions are controversial.

— The Cottingley Fairies, a series of trick photographs taken by two young British girls from 1917 to 1920.

— The alien autopsy film, supposedly footage of the examination of an extraterrestrial being which had purportedly died in the Roswell UFO incident. The film, presented by Ray Santilli in 1995, was later revealed to have been faked by Santilli and Gary Shoefield.

— In the late 1970s and early 1980s, photographer Robert B. Stein created convincing UFO photographs using only a Kodak Pocket InstaMatic camera and throwable discs, and claimed to be a contactee. His pictures appeared in many publications devoted to the paranormal. In 1985, he revealed how it was done.

— Rosie Ruiz finished first in the women's division of the 1980 Boston Marathon by riding the subway to a point near the finish line and jumping back into the race. Her marathon title was revoked when the hoax was discovered.

— The sale of the Eiffel Tower for scrap, an elaborate scam run twice by the master con artist Victor Lustig.

— American con artist George C. Parker made his living selling and re-selling public monuments in New York City.

— The Helius Project, about a non-existent alien being communicating with people on Earth, launched in 2003 and still online. Many people who interacted with Helius argue that Helius is real.

— Project Alpha, a hoax conceived by stage magician James Randi to fool psychic researchers.

— The Carlos hoax, another creation of The Amazing Randi, staged to discredit the New Age belief called trance channelling.

— The residents of Palisade, Nevada, once earned their living by pretending to be the "toughest town in the West". The violence was actually an elaborate show put on for tourists arriving on the train.

— Georg Paul Thomann, a fictional artist created by the group monochrom, who represented the Republic of Austria at the Sao Paulo Art Biennial. During the course of the event, no one had realized that the artist never really existed.

— The Priory of Sion (French:Prieuré de Sion), an alleged secret order sworn to defend the mythical Jesus bloodline which protected Jesus' descendants, including the Merovingian rulers of France and their heirs, was fabricated by French royalist Pierre Plantard in the 1950s as part of a personal plan to become King of France; fake documents created as part of the hoax have been included in best sellers purporting to be non-fiction such as The Holy Blood and the Holy Grail as well as novels such as Dan Brown's controversial The Da Vinci Code.

— The Paul is dead hoax of 1969 had it that the famous bassist of The Beatles was actually replaced after he had a fatal car accident in the late 1960s. "Clues" have been discovered by fans on different Beatles songs and album covers. This hoax was not started by The Beatles themselves (although they seemed to anticipate it in the song Glass Onion, released a year before the hoax took off), and Paul McCartney is one of the two Beatles still alive as of September 2007.

— Bonsai Kitten, an Internet hoax consisting of a fictional domain of a company that sold kittens inside jars as ornaments.

— In early summer 2006 an Internet hoax went around saying Jaleel White of the TV show Family Matters committed suicide, mirroring similar urban legends of other celebrity suicides and deaths.

— In what became known as the Berners Street Hoax in 1810, Theodore Hook tricked hundreds of people into showing up at 54 Berners Street, London.

— In 2006, A.N. Wilson was the victim of a hoax when he included a love letter by Sir John Betjeman in his biography of the poet. It turned out to be a fake letter with an acrostic that said "AN Wilson is a shit".

— In April, 1985, Sports Illustrated ran a profile written by George Plimpton of an amazing new pitching prospect for the New York Mets named Sidd Finch. Finch was a student of yoga ("Sidd" being short for "Siddhartha") who had studied with Tibetan monks to perfect his pitching and claimed to throw a 168 mph fastball. The Mets helped with the initial story but the magazine admitted to the hoax on April 15.

— Dead fairy hoax: On April 1, 2007, an illusion designer for magicians posted on his website some images illustrating the corpse of an unknown eight-inch creation, which was claimed to be the mummified remains of a fairy. He later sold the fairy on eBay for £280.

— De Grote Donorshow, a hoax reality television programme which was broadcast in the Netherlands on Friday, June 1, 2007 by BNN. The programme involved a supposedly terminally ill 37-year-old woman donating a kidney to one of three people requiring a kidney transplantation. Viewers were be able to send advice on who they think she should choose to give her kidney to via text messages. After the airing of the show, 50.000 people had requested a donor form.

12

Internet Slang

Internet slang/language is slang that Internet users have coined and promulgated. Such terms typically originated with the purpose of saving keystrokes, and many people use the same abbreviations in text messages. They are also very commonly used in instant messaging. The terms often appear in lower case, with capitals reserved for emphasis; for example, the pronoun "I" often appears simply as "i." People also use "u" to mean "you," and "r" to mean "are."

Like most jargon, Internet slang aggrandises authors and readers, causing them to appear to have specialised knowledge of a complex medium. However, there are cases where using Internet slang is considered ridiculous, due to association with the stereotype of the internet n00b.

Another feature common to Internet communication involves the truncation and morphing of words to forms that users can type more readily, and quickly. When new terms of internet slang are created, it takes time for them to become widely accepted. The small ring of friends using an instant messaging client most of the time is not enough. Web forums are a way to get new terminology out on the net, and accepted and used by a wide range of members of the internet community.

Internet slang words develop from common phrases that users simplify to be able to type faster. However, in games, new game players may try to emulate this, and unintentionally emphasize their own lack of knowledge through misuse of the terms and poor spelling. As a result, several internet slang abbreviations and spellings are most often used ironically. Players may use intentionally poor grammar and an excessive amount of leet (also written as 1337) speak to ridicule or satirise new players.

An example would be "pwned" (owned). "Pwned" means "beaten thoroughly"/"destroyed quickly and with ease" or "il ttyl, but that was funny 2 were i had 2 lmfao". Lmfao stands for "laughing my fucking ass off" and "ttyl" stand for "talk to you later". The word "Pwned" has been accepted as neolinguistic, and has been carried over into conversations.

The most common context of "pwned" is "pwned like a noob", meaning "destroyed with the quickness and ease with which one would destroy a new player". The use of this phrase, however, is looked upon as "nerdy," "arrogant," or "vulgar" (in the sense of the word meaning "unlearned and common") by some people.

Slang Classes

Abbreviations are probably the most used kind of internet slang in which a three- or four-letter abbreviation can be used instead of a string of words. For example, "LMAO" means "laughing my ass off" and "TTYL" means "Talk To You Later,", "LOL" generally stands for "Laughing Out Loud" (although it can signify "Lots of Laughs" or "Lots of Love") and "LOTI" stands for "Laughing On The Inside."

Abbreviations vary within internet groups, particularly for online games where each game's subculture develops its own terms. For example, in the online Massive multiplayer online role playing game (MMORPG) World of Warcraft, "AP" generally means "Attack Power" while in the MMORPG Maple Story it means "Ability Points." This can lead to considerable confusion for the new user. On popular, non-MMORPG, known as Neopets, almost all weapons have an abbrevation and these take a while to learn. One of the most famous would be SOS, meaning Sword of Skardsen (a popular weapon on Neopets)or meaning sorry or soz also meaning sorry.

In many cases these abbreviations may also be used as acronyms. Outside internet use, the abbreviation "LOL," signifying the pronunciation rather than the abbreviation, is finding its way into normal conversation, pronounced either ("ell oh ell") as an abbreviation or as an acronym ("lohl" or /l?l/).

The word "w00t" (pronounced woot) may be an acronym for "We Owned (beat severely) the Other Team," though other etymologies are also considered plausible. This is common in after-match chatrooms in team-based gaming servers where players can discuss the round after playing it. In conversational context, however, it means "hooray," "yay," "huzzah," or simply "What?" which is the original form of w00t.

Emoticons

Emoticons—also known as smileys—are a form of ASCII art where a short sequence of printable characters is used to resemble a facial expression and convey an emotion. The basic smiley is :), where the colon or number 8 represents the eyes and the parenthesis the mouth, forming a rough approximation of a "happy face". Other common emoticons or "smileys" are those showing if one is sad :(, or if one is shocked 8-O. Emoticons may be more easily recognised by tilting one's head to the left, and a great many variants exist, such as 8D, =), =D, =>), >=D,:p, |=[, >8), >XD, XP,|8[,8-0,]=(:). There is another variation of "smileys" resembling a wink by combining a semicolon and a parenthesis, such as ;), ;] or ;}. The differing use of parentheses can give the emoticon a slightly different slant; for example ;} can represent an evil or otherwise malicious wink.

The other major style of emoticon, which does not require the viewer to tilt their head, evolved in East Asia. In the basic smiling manga emoticon, ^_^, the carets representing the eyes, and the underscore a mouth. Notably, this "smiley" has a straight mouth and smiling eyes, suggesting a cultural difference in reading emotions. Another popular east Asian emoticon is (^?^), using a Japanese character to represent the nose. Kirby can also be done, (>'.')>, and a variety of other emoticons can be created in this form, such as -_-, o_o, #_# and ^-^;, @(^.^)@(monkey), <><(fish), }{}(fish) all which signify different emotions, and also, judging by the font used in the chatroom, others can be made, including

§, which could mean different things, judging by the way the text forms the symbol, and in Wikipedia's case, it is a 'gas mask' effect

Emoticons most probably found their origins in the early days of e-mail as a method of avoiding a potentially embarrassing or emotionally damaging misunderstanding by clarifying intent, similar to the slang jk, meaning just kidding.

'n00b'

The word "n00b" is used in internet slang coming from the word "newbie." Generally, the term "newb" is used endearingly for a newcomer to a game or commonplace.

However, "noob" is an insulting word aimed at someone who has persisted in an environment but is being ridiculed for lack of skill and/or knowledge of the environment. There are also many variations of the word "noob", such as "nub", "naab", "fr00b", "ch00b", "n00b", "Narb", "fr33b", "n33b", etc. but it is not to be confused with the mostly non-offensive "newb."

In some places, such as popular MMORPG's or forums, this can be attributed to someone who has been in a certain place for a long time and retains their ignorance. The term "n00b" can be used describe a person who maintains an attitude of stupidity, whereas a "newbie" is more likely to be used in describing someone who is simply ignorant or inexperienced.

The term "newbie" is usually regarded as less of an insult than "noob." Newb is generally reserved for a person who is simply new to a game/topic and has not yet full understanding of its working. Noob is used to classify someone who has persisted in a game/topic and still acts poorly, whether in skill or demeanor. There are also many ways people can joke around with the word "noob", example, if someone does something dumb, and another player will joke around saying "Haha, you choob".

Variation of Tagging

A variation of tagging meant to resemble XML or HTML code is used to give emphasis on posts on blogs, forums, or message boards. For example, in HTML, when "<b>" and "</b>" are placed around text, a web browser will display it in boldface. Because emotions and inflection do not apply to text, Internet users will use custom XML tags for such emphasis, such as "<sarcasm>..</sarcasm>" "<rant>..</rant>" or "<white lie>..</white lie>". These "tags" are often meant to be generally humorous or informative. The opening tag may also sometimes be omitted when a block of text's designation as such is not meant to be known at first, such as when a sarcastic comment is made and only after the reader finishes it do they see the closing </sarcasm> tag and realise the intent of the message. Fake BB-codes are similarly used.

SLANG TERMS

Slang is the use of highly informal words and expressions that are not considered standard in the speaker's dialect or language. Slang is often highly regional, specific to a particular territory. Slang terms are frequently particular to a certain subculture, such as musicians, and members of minority groups. Nevertheless, usage of slang expressions can spread outside their original arenas to become commonly understood, such as "cool" and "jive".

While some words eventually lose their status as slang, others continue to be considered as such by most speakers. In spite of this, the process tends to lead the original users to replace the words with other, less-recognised terms to maintain group identity.

Jargon

Being informal speech, slang should be distinguished from jargon, which is the technical vocabulary of a particular profession. Moreover, jargon may not be intended to exclude nongroup members from the conversation, but rather deals with technical peculiarities of a given field requiring a specialised vocabulary.

According to Bethany K. Dumas and Jonathan Lighter, an expression should be considered "true slang" if it meets at least two of the following criteria:

— It lowers, if temporarily, "the dignity of formal or serious speech or writing"; in other words, it is likely to be seen in such contexts as a "glaring misuse of register."

— Its use implies that the user is familiar with whatever is referred to, or with a group of people that are familiar with it and use the term.

— "It is a taboo term in ordinary discourse with people of a higher social status or greater responsibility."

— It replaces "a well known conventional synonym." This is done primarily to avoid "the discomfort caused by the conventional item [or by] further elaboration."

One use of slang is to circumvent social taboos, as mainstream language tends to shy away from evoking certain realities. For this reason, slang vocabularies are particularly rich in certain domains, such as sexuality, violence, crime and drugs.

Alternatively, slang can grow out of mere familiarity with the things described. Among wine connoisseurs, Cabernet Sauvignon might be known as "Cab Sav", Chardonnay as "Chard" and so on; this means that naming the different wines expends less superfluous effort. It also serves as a shared code among connoisseurs.

Even within a single language community, slang tends to vary widely across social, ethnic, economic, and geographic strata. Slang sometimes grows more and more common until it becomes the dominant way of saying something, at which time it is regarded as mainstream, acceptable language (e.g. the Spanish word caballo), while at other times it may fall into disuse. Numerous slang terms pass into informal mainstream speech, and sometimes into formal speech, though this may involve a change in meaning or usage. Slang very often involves the creation of novel meanings for existing words. It is very common for such novel meanings to diverge significantly from the standard meaning. Thus, "cool" and "hot" can both mean "very good, impressive or good looking."

Slang terms are often only known within the people that it belongs too. For example, Leet Speak (Leet or "1337") is popular among online video gamers (although it is slowly being picked up by gaming in general). Text language is also a different form of slang used among people to shorten words when typing.

SMS Language

SMS language (also known as chatspeak, txt, txtspk, texting language or txt talk) is the English language slang used in mobile phone SMS. It is an abbreviated form of English known as a rebus. With predictive text input increasingly being used, it is becoming less common.

It is similar to AOL speak, and it evolved from the shorthand used in Internet chatrooms to accommodate the small number of characters allowed (early SMS permitted only 160 characters), and as a convenient language for the small keyboards on mobile phones. Without practice, sending SMS messages can be time consuming. The objective of txt is to use the fewest number of characters needed to put across a comprehensible message. Hence, punctuation and grammar are largely ignored.

Txt Devices

Single letters can replace words. Examples:

— be becomes b

— see becomes c

— are becomes r

— you becomes u

— why becomes y

— in becomes n

Single digits can replace words. Examples:

— ate becomes 8

— for becomes 4

— to or too becomes 2

A single letter or digit can replace a syllable. Examples:

— ate becomes 8, so:

  — activate becomes activ8

  — great becomes GR8

  — mate becomes m8

  — later becomes l8r/l8a

  — plates becomes pl8s

  — skater becomes sk8r/sk8a

— for or Fore becomes 4, so:

  — before becomes (combining both of the above) b4

  — therefore becomes der4

There are miscellaneous adaptations of characters. Examples:

However, these are fairly uncommon for the pure reason that they take even longer to type than the originals for the average typist.

— ss becomes $

— oo becomes %

— '-orr-' becomes '-oz'

  — For example, Sorry becomes Soz, and Tomorrow

becomes Tomoz (further abbreviated to 2moz and later to 2mz).

Combinations of the above can shorten a single or multiple words. Example:

— your and you are both become ur

Characters and punctuation are removed to shorten messages:

— Vowels are removed such that the sequence of consonants remain and the word is still recognisable.
  — For example, between becomes btwn, homework becomes "hmwk", and "yearbook" becomes "yrbk".
— Whole words may be omitted, especially articles.
— Punctuation may be removed; only question mark and exclamation marks are generally used. The space and capital letter is often omitted after a period. "/" signifies abbreviation, such as "w/" for "with" and "s/t" for "something".

Other transcriptions of slang or dialect terms can be used if shorter than the original words, as in cos (with fewer letters than because.)

Instant Messaging

Instant messaging (IM) is a form of real-time communication between two or more people based on typed text. The text is conveyed via computers connected over a network such as the Internet.

Instant messaging requires an instant messaging client that connects to an instant messaging service. Instant messaging differs from e-mail in that conversations happen in real-time. A multiprotocol instant messaging application allows one client to connect to multiple IM networks.

Instant messaging services owe many ideas to an older and still popular online chat medium named Internet Relay Chat (IRC). In early instant messaging programmes, each letter appeared when it was typed, and when letters were deleted to correct typos this was also seen in real time. This made it more like a telephone conversation than exchanging letters.

In modern instant messaging programmes, the other party in the conversation generally only sees each line of text right after a new line is started. Most instant messaging applications also include the ability to set a status message, roughly analogous to the message on a telephone answering machine.

Benefits of Instant Messaging

Instant messaging offers real-time communication and allows easy collaboration, which might be considered more akin to genuine conversation than email's "letter" format. In contrast to e-mail, the parties know whether the peer is available. Most systems allow the user to set an online status or away message so peers are notified when the user is available, busy, or away from the computer.

On the other hand, people are not forced to reply immediately to incoming messages. For this reason, some people consider communication via instant messaging to be less intrusive than communication via phone. However, some systems allow the sending of messages to people not currently logged on (offline messages), thus removing much of the difference between IM and email.

Instant messaging allows instantaneous communication between a number of parties simultaneously, by transmitting information quickly and efficiently, featuring immediate receipt of acknowledgment or reply. In certain cases IM involves additional features, which make it even more popular, i.e. to see the other party, e.g. by using web-cams, or to talk directly for free over the internet.

It is possible to save a conversation for later reference. Instant messages are typically logged in a local message history which closes the gap to the persistent nature of e-mails and facilitates quick exchange of information like URLs or document snippets (which can be unwieldy when communicated via telephone).

Orgine of Instant Messaging

Instant messaging applications began to appear in the 1970s on multi-user operating systems like UNIX, initially to facilitate communication with other users logged in to the same machine, then on the local network, and subsequently across the Internet. Some of these used a peer-to-peer protocol (eg talk, ntalk and ytalk), while others required peers to connect to a server. Because all of these protocols were based inside a console window, most of those discovering the Internet in the mid-1990s and equating it with the web tended not to encounter them.

In the last half of the 1980s and into the early 1990s, the Quantum Link online service for Commodore 64 computers offered user-to-user messages between currently connected customers which they called "On-Line Messages" (or OLM for short). Quantum Link's better known later incarnation, America Online, offers a similar product under the name "AOL Instant Messages" (AIM).

While the Quantum Link service ran on a Commodore 64, using only the Commodore's PETSCII text-graphics, the screen was visually divided up into sections and OLMs would appear as a yellow bar saying

"Message From:" and the name of the sender along with the message across the top of whatever the user was already doing, and presented a list of options for responding. As such, it could be considered a sort of GUI, albeit much more primitive than the later Unix, Windows and Macintosh based GUI IM programmes. OLMs were what Q-Link called "Plus Services" meaning they charged an extra per-minute fee on top of the monthly Q-Link access costs.

Modern, Internet-wide, GUI-based messaging clients, as they are known today, began to take off in the mid 1990s with ICQ (1996) being the first, followed by AOL Instant Messenger (AOL Instant Messenger, 1997). AOL later acquired Mirabilis, the creators of ICQ. A few years later ICQ (by now owned by AOL) was awarded two patents for instant messaging by the U.S. patent office. Meanwhile, other companies developed their own applications (Yahoo, MSN, Excite, Ubique, IBM), each with its own proprietary protocol and client; users therefore had to run multiple client applications if they wished to use more than one of these networks.

In 2000, an open source application and open standards-based protocol called Jabber was launched. Jabber servers could act as gateways to other IM protocols, reducing the need to run multiple clients. Modern multi-protocol clients such as Pidgin, Trillian, Adium and Miranda can use any of the popular IM protocols without the need for a server gateway.

Recently, many instant messaging services have begun to offer video conferencing features, Voice Over IP (VoIP) and web conferencing services. Web conferencing services integrate both video conferencing and instant messaging capabilities. Some newer instant messaging companies are offering desktop sharing, IP radio, and IPTV to the voice and video features.

The term "instant messenger" is a service mark of Time Warner and may not be used in software not affiliated with AOL in the United States. For this reason, the instant messaging client formerly known as Gaim or gaim announced in April 2007 that they would be renamed "Pidgin".

Cooperation

There have been several attempts to create a unified standard for instant messaging: IETF's SIP (Session Initiation Protocol) and SIMPLE (SIP for Instant Messaging and Presence Leveraging Extensions), APEX (Application Exchange), Prim (Presence and Instant Messaging Protocol), the open XML-based XMPP (Extensible Messaging and Presence Protocol), more commonly known as Jabber and OMA's (Open Mobile Alliance) IMPS (Instant Messaging and Presence Service) created specifically for mobile devices.

Most attempts at creating a unified standard for the major IM providers (AOL, Yahoo! and Microsoft) have failed and each continues to use its own proprietary protocol.

However, while discussions at IETF were stalled, Reuters head of collaboration services, David Gurle (the founder of Microsoft's Real Time Communication and Collaboration business), surprised everybody by signing the first inter-service provider connectivity agreement on September 2003.

This historic agreement enabled AIM, ICQ and MSN Messenger users to talk with Reuters Messaging counterparts and vice-versa against an access fee. Following this breakthrough agreement between networks Microsoft, Yahoo! and AOL came to a deal where Microsoft's Live Communication Server 2005 (which is interestingly also used by Reuters for its Reuters Messaging service) users would also have the possibility to talk to public instant messaging users. This deal settled once for all the protocol for interconnectivity in the market as SIP/SIMPLE and established a connectivity fee for accessing public instant messaging clouds.

Separately, on October 13, 2005 Microsoft and Yahoo! announced that by (the Northern Hemisphere) summer of 2006 they would interoperate using SIP/SIMPLE which is followed on December 2005 by the AOL and Google strategic partnership deal where Google Talk users would be able to talk with AIM and ICQ users provided they have an identity at AOL.

There are two ways to combine the many disparate protocols:

— One way is to combine the many disparate protocols inside the IM client application.

— The other way is to combine the many disparate protocols inside the IM server application. This approach moves the task of communicating to the other services to the server. Clients need not know or care about other IM protocols. For example, LCS 2005 Public IM Connectivity. This approach is popular in Jabber/XMPP servers however the so-called transport projects suffer the same reverse engineering difficulties as any other project involved with closed protocols or formats.

Some approaches, such as that adopted by the Sonork enterprise IM software or the Jabber/XMPP network or Winpopup LAN Messenger, allow organisations to create their own private instant messaging network by enabling them to limit access to the server (often with the IM network entirely behind their firewall) and administer user permissions. Other corporate messaging systems allow registered users to also connect from outside the corporation LAN, by using a secure firewall-friendly HTTPS based protocol. Typically, a dedicated corporate IM server has several advantages such as pre-populated contact lists, integrated authentication, and better security and privacy.

Some networks have made changes to prevent them from being utilised by such multi-network IM clients. For example, Trillian had to release several revisions and patches to allow its users to access the MSN, AOL, and Yahoo! networks, after changes were made to these networks. The major IM providers typically cite the need for formal agreements as well as security concerns as reasons for making these changes.

Mobile Instant Messaging (MIM)

Mobile Instant Messaging (MIM) is a presence enabled messaging service that aims to transpose the desktop messaging experience to the usage scenario of being on the move.

While several of the core ideas of the desktop experience on one hand apply to a connected mobile device, others do not: Users usually only look at their phone's screen—presence status changes might occur under different circumstances as happens at the desktop, and several functional limits exist based on the fact that the vast majority of mobile communication devices are chosen by their users to fit into the palm of their hand.

Some of the form factor and mobility related differences need to be taken into account in order to create a really adequate, powerful and yet convenient mobile experience: radio bandwidth, memory size, availability of media formats, keypad based input, screen output, CPU performance and battery power are core issues that desktop device users and even nomadic users with connected notebooks are usually not exposed to.

Several formerly untackled issues have been identified and addressed within IMPS, which was developed as part of an early mobile telephone industry initiative to kick off a broader usage of mobile instant messaging. The Open Mobile Alliance has taken over this standard, formerly called Wireless Village, as IMPS V1.0 in November 2002. Since then this standards has been further developed to IMPS V1.3, the latest candidate for release, and is expected to be released before the end of 2006.

There are downloadable mobile applications offered by different independent developers that allow users to chat within public (MSN, Yahoo!, Google Talk, AIM, ICQ) and corporate (LCS, Sametime, Reuters) IM services from mobile devices.

Among the advantages of using such IM clients over SMS are: IM clients use data instead of SMS text messages; IM-like chat mode, faster and quicker messaging. Some IM software allows group communication. Several large scale mobile telephone industry companies are planning to jointly deliver a ubiquitous, interoperable presence enabled messaging service, built according to interoperability recommendations developed in the GSM Association. Considering these organisations are jointly representing approximately 1.5 billion active Short Text Messaging (SMS) users, it remains to be seen [vague] if such an initiative may also help to drive the different industry factions to agree on a truly interoperable approach at least for Mobile Instant Messaging sometime in the not too far future.

In the meantime, other developments have proposed usage of downloadable applications with the intention to create their own approach to IM that runs on most mobile phones worldwide. Essentially, several of these clients are Java applications are instantly downloaded and then connected to back-end servers through GPRS/3G Internet Channels. Some of the implementations can connect to other IM services.

Effects on People with an Auditory

Instant messaging opens new methods of spontaneous communication for people that have an impairment in hearing, auditory processing, or speech. It is considered by many a powerful way to allow equal opportunities in communication, without the aid of special devices or services designed for users with hearing loss.

Friend-to-Friend Networks

Instant Messaging may be done in a Friend-to-friend network, in which each node connects to the friends on the friendslist. This allows for communication with friends of friends and for the building of chatrooms for instant messages with all friends on that network.

Business Application

Instant messaging has proven to be similar to personal computers, e-mail, and the WWW, in that its adoption for use as a business communications medium was driven primarily by individual employees using consumer software at work, rather than by formal mandate or provisioning by corporate information technology departments. Tens of millions of the consumer IM accounts in use are being used for business purposes by employees of companies and other organisations.

In response to the demand for business-grade IM and the need to ensure security and legal compliance, a new type of instant messaging, called "Enterprise Instant Messaging" ("EIM") was created when Lotus Software launched Lotus Sametime in 1999. Microsoft followed suit shortly thereafter with Microsoft Exchange Instant Messaging, and later created a new platform called Microsoft Office Live Communications Server.

Since then, both IBM Lotus and Microsoft have introduced federation between their EIM systems and some of the public IM networks thus employees may use a single interface to both their internal EIM system and their buddies on AOL, MSN, and Yahoo!. Current leading EIM platforms include IBM Lotus Sametime, Microsoft Office Live Communications Server, and Jabber XCP.

The adoption of IM across corporate networks outside of the control of IT organisations creates many risks and liabilities for companies who do not effectively manage and support IM use. Companies implement specialised IM archiving and security products and services like those from Secure Computing, Akonix, Surfcontrol, and ScanSafe to mitigate these risks and provide safe, secure, productive instant messaging capabilities to their employees.

On the other hand, the informal usage of instant messaging by the younger generation has also affected the quality of messages as these youngsters adapt the habits that they are used to in instant messaging into the workplace. The tendency to misspell, the use of informal language, emoticons and the shortening of longer or commonly used words whilst casual chatting online with friends might unconsciously seep into the more formal and serious conversations in the workplace. Although instant messaging has made it more convenient for faster relaying of messages, certain guidelines and etiquette rules should be observed to fully utilise the usability of this important tool.

Risks and Liabilities

Although instant messaging delivers many benefits, it also carries with it certain risks and liabilities, particularly when used in workplaces, although there are not that many at all. Among these are:

— Security risks (e.g. IM used to infect computers with spyware, viruses, trojans, worms)

— Compliance risks

— Inappropriate use

— Intellectual property leakage

Hackers' use of instant messaging networks to deliver malicious code has grown consistently from 2004 to the present, with the number of discrete attacks listed by the IM Security Center having grown 15% from 347 attacks in 2005 to 406 in 2006. Hackers use two methods of delivering malicious code through IM: delivery of virus, trojan, or spyware within an infected file, and the use of "socially engineered" text with a web address that entices the recipient to click on a URL that connects him or her to a website that then downloads malicious code.

Viruses, worms, and trojans typically propagate by sending themselves rapidly through the infected user's buddy list. An effective attack using a "poison URL" may reach tens of thousands of people in minutes when each person's buddy list receives messages appearing to be from a trusted friend. The recipients click on the web address, and the entire cycle starts again. Infections may range from nuisance to criminal, and are becoming more sophisticated each year.

In addition to the malicious code threat, the use of instant messaging at work also creates a risk of non-compliance to laws and regulations governing the use of electronic communications in businesses. In the United States alone there are over 10,000 laws and regulations related to electronic messaging and records retention. The more well-known of these include the Sarbanes-Oxley Act, HIPAA, and SEC 17a-3. Recent changes to Federal Rules of Civil Procedure, effective December 1, 2006, create a new category for electronic records which may be requested during discovery (law) in legal proceedings.

Most countries around the world also regulate the use of electronic messaging and electronic records retention in similar fashion to the United States. The most common regulations related to IM at work involve the need to produce archived business communications to satisfy government or judicial requests under law. Many instant messaging communications fall into the category of business communications that must be archived and retrievable.

Organisations of all types must protect themselves from the liability of their employees' inappropriate use of IM. The informal, immediate, and ostensibly anonymous nature of instant messaging makes it a candidate for abuse in the workplace. The topic of inappropriate IM use became front page news in October 2006 when Congressman Mark Foley resigned his seat after admitting sending offensive instant messages of a sexual nature to underage former House pages from his Congressional office PC. The Mark Foley Scandal led to media coverage and mainstream newspaper articles warning of the risks of inappropriate IM use in workplaces.

In most countries, corporations have a legal responsibility to ensure harassment-free work environment for employees. The use of corporate-owned computers, networks, and software to harass an individual or spread inappropriate jokes or language creates a liability for not only the offender but also the employer. A survey by IM archiving and security provider Akonix Systems, Inc. in March 2007 showed that 31% of respondents had been harassed over IM at work. Companies now include instant messaging as an integral component of their policies on appropriate use of the World Wide Web, email, and other corporate assets.

Security and Archiving

In the early 2000s, a new class of IT security provider emerged to provide remedies for the risks and liabilities faced by corporations who chose to use IM for business communications. The IM security providers created new products to be installed in corporate networks for the purpose of archiving, content-scanning, and security-scanning IM traffic moving in and out of the corporation. Similar to the e-mail filtering vendors, the IM security providers focus on the risks and liabilities described above.

With rapid adoption of IM in the workplace, demand for IM security products began to grow in the mid-2000s. By 2007, the preferred platform for the purchase of security software had become the "appliance", according to IDC, who estimate that by 2008, 80% of network security products will be delivered via an appliance.

Some instant messaging systems are distributed among many different instances and thus difficult to measure in total (e.g. Jabber). While some numbers are given by the owners of a complete instant messaging system, others are provided by commercial vendors of a part of a distributed system. Some companies may be motivated to inflate their numbers in order to increase advertisement earnings or to attract partners, clients, or customers. Importantly, some numbers are reported as the number of "active" users (without a shared standard of that activity), others indicate total user accounts, while others indicate only the users logged in during an instance of peak usage.

— AIM: 53 million active users (September 2006), "over 100 million" total (January 2006).

— Jabber: between 40 and 50 million (January 2007). Note that this number is based on calculations of Jabber Inc ("nearly 10 million open source users") which differ from those of Process-One ("Our total deployments account for more than 20 millions of accounts"). Process-One is a company providing services based on the Jabber server software ejabberd. Accordingly, as there are many other open source servers (some also with companies behind it), the number provided by Jabber Inc is probably too small. If we presume ejabberd has a 40% market share amongst public and non-public open source server deployments, there are 50 million users using an open source server. This would mean, including Jabber Inc's numbers, that there are around 90 million Jabber users instead of 50 million.

Jargon

Jargon is terminology that relates to a specific activity, profession or group. Much like slang it develops as a kind of shorthand, to express ideas that are frequently discussed between members of a group. In many cases a standard term may be given a more precise or specialised usage among practicioners of a field.

Jargon is used in several fields:

— sports: one can find jargon just by watching a major league baseball broadcast, where commentators compete for the greatest density of technical sport terms and other sport-related metaphors.

— medicine: Particularly in the operating room or under emergency conditions, particular jargons have developed that allow medical professionals to communicate quickly and effectively where common language would take much longer. This kind of jargon is also known as technical terminology.

— information technology and the Internet created many overlapping jargons used by computer scientists, programmers, system architects, nerds, geeks and hackers to communicate. The proper usage of these words is a prerequisite for inclusion in these groups.

— nautical terms are an ancient form of jargon.

Pitfalls of jargon

In some cases it is used to distinguish those belonging to a group from those who are not. This is sometimes called "guild" or "insider" jargon. Those unfamiliar with a subject can often be tagged by their incorrect use of jargon. The use of jargon by outsiders is considered by insiders to be audacious, since it constitutes a claim to membership of the insider group. Jargon often comes across as pedantic, nerdy, and divorced from meaning to outsiders.

13

E-mail Spam

E-mail Spam, also known as bulk e-mail or junk e-mail is a subset of spam that involves sending nearly identical messages to numerous recipients by e-mail. A common synonym for spam is unsolicited bulk e-mail (UBE). Some definitions of spam specifically include the aspects of email that is unsolicited and sent in bulk. UCE refers specifically to Unsolicited Commercial E-mail.

From the beginning of the internet, sending of junk e-mail has been prohibited, enforced by ISPs Terms of Service/Acceptable Use Policy (ToS/AUP) and peer pressure. Even with a thousand users, using junk e-mail for advertising is not tenable, and with a million users it is not only not practical, but very expensive as well, costing US businesses on the order of $10 billion per year in 2003. As the internet has grown, ISP's have no longer been able to effectively police the sending of UBE and have turned to government for relief, which has failed to materialize, particularly in the US, which aborted tough state laws with a promiscuous federal law, the CAN-SPAM Act of 2003, although some countries have passed laws against spam, especially in Europe and Australia.

As the recipient directly bears the cost of delivery, storage, and processing, one could regard spam as the electronic equivalent of "postage-due" junk mail. Due to the low cost of sending unsolicited e-mail and the potential profit entailed only enforcing an opt-in law will stop junk e-mail. "Today, much of the spam volume is sent by career criminals and malicious hackers who won't stop until they're all rounded up and put in jail."

Spam is rarely sent by well-known companies, and is quickly regretted; spam from these sources is sometimes called main sleaze. A widely-known instance of spamming by a large corporation was Kraft Foods' marketing of its Gevalia coffee brand. Another more recent offender was the company iDate, which used e-mail harvesting directed at subscribers to the Quechup website to spam their friends and contacts.

Advance fee fraud spam such as the Nigerian "419" scam may be sent by a single individual from a cyber cafe in a developing country. Organized "spam gangs" operating from Russia or eastern Europe share many features in common with other forms of organized crime, including turf battles and revenge killings. As much as 80% of spam received by internet users in North America and Europe can be traced to fewer than 600 spammers.

Spammers may engage in deliberate fraud to send out their messages. Spammers often use false names, addresses, phone numbers, and other contact information to set up "disposable" accounts at various Internet service providers. They also often use falsified or stolen credit card numbers to pay for these accounts. This allows them to move quickly from one account to the next as the host ISPs discover and shut down each one.

Spam is also a medium for fraudsters to scam users to enter personal information on fake Web sites using e-mail forged to look like it is from a bank or other organization such as Paypal. This is known as phishing.

Senders may go to great lengths to conceal the origin of their messages. Large companies may hire another firm to send their messages so that complaints or blocking of email falls on a third party. Others engage in spoofing of e-mail addresses (much easier than IP address spoofing). The e-mail protocol (SMTP) has no authentication by default, so the spammer can pretend to originate a message apparently from any e-mail address. To prevent this, some ISPs and domains require the use of SMTP-AUTH, allowing positive identification of the specific account from which an e-mail originates.

Senders cannot completely spoof e-mail delivery chains (the 'Received' header), since the receiving mailserver records the actual connection from the last mailserver's IP address. To counter this, some spammers forge additional delivery headers to make it appear as if the e-mail had previously traversed many legitimate servers.

Spoofing can have serious consequences for legitimate e-mail users. Not only can their e-mail inboxes get clogged up with "undeliverable" e-mails in addition to volumes of spam, they can mistakenly be identified as a spammer. Not only may they receive irate e-mail from spam victims, but (if spam victims report the e-mail address owner to the ISP, for example) a naïve ISP may terminate their service for spamming.

Spammers frequently seek out and make use of vulnerable third-party systems such as open mail relays and open proxy servers. SMTP forwards mail from one server to another-mail servers that ISPs run commonly require some form of authentication to ensure that the user is a customer of that ISP. Open relays, however, do not properly check who is using the mail server and pass all mail to the destination address, making it harder to track down spammers.

Increasingly, spammers use networks of malware-infected PCs (zombies) to send their spam. Zombie networks are also known as Botnets (such zombifying malware is known as a bot, short for robot). In June 2006, an estimated 80% of e-mail spam were sent by zombie PCs, an increase of 30% from the prior year. An estimated 55 billion e-mail spam were sent each day in June 2006, an increase of 25 billion per day from June 2005.

Statistics and Estimates

Growth of E-mail Spam

Spam is growing, with no signs of abating. The amount of spam users see in their mailboxes is just the tip of the iceberg, since spammers' lists often contain a large percentage of invalid addresses and many spam filters simply delete or reject "obvious spam".

In absolute numbers

— 1978 - An e-mail spam is sent to 600 addresses.

— 1994 - First large-scale spam sent to 6000 newsgroups, reaching millions of people.

— 2005 - (June) 30 billion per day

— 2006 - (June) 55 billion per day

— 2006 - (December) 85 billion per day

— 2007 - (February) 90 billion per day

As a percentage of the total volume of e-mail

MAAWG estimates that 80-85% of incoming mail is "abusive email", as of the last quarter of 2005. The sample size for the MAAWG's study was over 100 million mailboxes.

Highest amount of spam received

According to Steve Ballmer, Microsoft founder Bill Gates receives four million e-mails per year, most of them being spam. At the same time Jef Poskanzer, owner of the domain name acme.com, was receiving over one million spam emails per day.

Source of spam

Origin or source of spam refers to the geographical location of the computer from which the spam is sent; it is not the country where the spammer resides, nor the country that hosts the spamvertised site. Due to the international nature of spam, often the spammer, the hijacked spam-sending computer, the spamvertised server, and the user target of the spam are all located in different countries.

In terms of volume of spam: According to Sophos, the major sources of spam in the second quarter of 2007 (April to June) were the United States (the origin of 19.6% of spam messages), followed by China (8.4%) and South Korea (6.5%). When grouped by continents, spam comes mostly from Asia (35,2%), Europe (28,5%) and North America (24,2%). Overall volume has increased 9% in the last year.

In terms of number of IP addresses: The Spamhaus Project (which measures spam sources in terms of number of IP addresses used for spamming, rather than volume of spam sent) ranks the top three as the United States, China, and Russia, with South Korea placed at #6 behind Japan and Canada.

In terms of networks: As of 5 June 2007, the three networks hosting the most spammers are Verizon, AT&T, and VSNL International. Verizon inherited many of these spam sources from its acquisition of MCI, specifically through the UUNet subsidiary of MCI, which Verizon subsequently renamed Verizon Business.

Spamvertised sites

Most spam contains a URL to a website. According to a Commtouch report in June 2004, "only five countries are hosting 99.68% of the global spammer websites", of which the foremost is China, hosting 73.58% of all web sites referenced within spam.

Most common products advertised

According to information compiled by Spam-Filter-Review.com, E-mail spam for 2006 can be broken down as follows.

E-Mail Spam by Category	
Products	25%
Financial	20%
Adult	19%
Scams	9%
Health	7%
Internet	7%
Leisure	6%
Spiritual	4%
Other	3%

Pornography alone accounted for 2.5 billion daily emails sent in 2006, equating to 4.5 daily porn emails per person.

Legality of Spam

Sending spam violates the Acceptable Use Policy (AUP) of almost all Internet Service Providers. Providers vary in their willingness or ability to enforce their AUP; some actively enforce their terms, some lack adequate personnel or technical skills for enforcement, while others may be reluctant to enforce restrictive terms against otherwise profitable customers.

In the United States spam is legally permissible according to the CAN-SPAM Act of 2003, provided it follows certain criteria: a truthful subject line; no false information in the technical headers or sender address; "conspicuous" display of the postal address of the sender; and other minor requirements. If the spam fails to comply with any of these requirements, then it is illegal. Aggravated or accelerated penalties apply if the spammer harvested the email addresses using methods described earlier.

Article 13 of the European Union Directive on Privacy and Electronic Communications (2002/58/EC) provides that the EU member states shall take appropriate measures to ensure that unsolicited communications for the purposes of direct marketing are not allowed either without the consent of the subscribers concerned or in respect of subscribers who do not wish to receive these communications, the choice between these options to be determined by national legislation.

In Australia, the relevant legislation is the Spam Act 2003 which covers some types of e-mail and phone spam, which took effect on 11 April 2004. Unlike the Can Spam Act (US)(opt-out), the Spam Act (AUS) provides that "Unsolicited commercial electronic messages must not be sent" (opt-in). Penalties are up to 10,000 penalty units (AUS $110 per penalty unit), approximately USD 900,000, or 2,000 penalty units for a person other than a body corporate.

The use of botnets can be perceived as theft. The spammer consumes a zombie owner's bandwidth and resources without any cost. In addition, spam is perceived as theft of services. The receiving SMTP servers consume significant amounts of system resources dealing with this unwanted traffic. As a result, service providers have to spend large amounts of money to make their systems capable of handling these amounts of email. Such costs are inevitably passed on to the service providers' customers.

Accessing privately owned computer resources without the owner's permission counts as illegal under computer crime statutes in most nations. Deliberate spreading of computer viruses is also illegal in the United States and elsewhere. Thus, some common behaviors of spammers are criminal regardless of the legality of spamming per se. Even before the advent of laws specifically banning or regulating spamming, spammers were successfully prosecuted under computer fraud and abuse laws for wrongfully using others' computers.

Legislative efforts to curb spam have been ineffective or counterproductive. For example, the CAN-SPAM Act of 2003 requires that each message include a means to "opt out" (i.e., decline future e-mail from the same source). It is widely believed that responding to opt-out requests is unwise, as this merely confirms to the spammer that they have reached an active e-mail account. If this is true, the CAN-SPAM Act's opt-out provisions are counterproductive in two ways: first, recipients who are aware of the potential risks of opting out will decline to do so; second, attempts to opt-out provide spammers with useful information on their targets. A 2002 study by the Center for Democracy and Technology found that about 16% of web sites tested with opt-out requests continued to spam.

Anti-spam techniques

The US Department of Energy Computer Incident

Advisory Committee (CIAC) has provided specific countermeasures against electronic mail spamming. Some popular methods for filtering and refusing spam include e-mail filtering based on the content of the e-mail, DNS-based blackhole lists (DNSBL), greylisting, spamtraps, enforcing technical requirements, checksumming systems to detect bulk email, and by putting some sort of cost on the sender via a Proof-of-work system or a micropayment. Each method has strengths and weaknesses and each is controversial due to its weaknesses.

Detecting spam based on the content of the e-mail, either by detecting keywords such as "viagra" or by statistical means, is very popular. Such methods can be very accurate when they are correctly tuned to the types of legitimate email that an individual gets, but they can also make mistakes such as detecting the keyword "cialis" in the word "specialist". The content also doesn't determine whether the email was either unsolicited or bulk, the two key features of spam. So, if a friend sends you a joke that mentions "viagra", content filters can easily mark it as being spam even though it is both solicited and not bulk.

The most popular DNSBLs are lists of IP addresses of known spammers, open relays, zombie spammers etc. Spamtraps are often email addresses that were never valid or have been invalid for a long time that are used to collect spam. An effective spamtrap is not announced and is only found by dictionary attacks or by pulling addresses off hidden webpages. For a spamtrap to remain effective the address must never be given to anyone. Some black lists, such as spamcop, use spamtraps to catch spammers and blacklist them.

Enforcing technical requirements of the Simple Mail Transfer Protocol (SMTP) can be used to block mail coming from systems that are not compliant with the RFC standards. A lot of spammers use poorly written software or are unable to comply with the standards because they do not have legitimate control of the computer sending spam (zombie computer). So by setting restrictions on the mail transfer agent (MTA) a mail administrator can reduce spam significantly. In many situations, simply requiring a valid fully qualified domain name (FQDN) in the SMTP's EHLO (extended hello) statement is enough to block 25% of incoming spam. Some small organizations go so far as to remove their MX (Mail eXchange) record and arrange to have their A-record point to their SMTP server. RFC standards call for fall-back to a domain's A record when an MX lookup fails. While this method runs the risk of losing some legitimate e-mail from being received, some claim that it results in a 75% reduction in spam.

E-mail Address Harvesting

In order to send spam, spammers need to obtain the e-mail addresses of the intended recipients. To this end, both spammers themselves and list merchants gather huge lists of potential e-mail addresses. Since spam is, by definition, unsolicited, this address harvesting is done without the consent (and sometimes against the expressed will) of the address owners. As a consequence, spammers' address lists are inaccurate. A single spam run may target tens of millions of possible addresses — many of which are invalid, malformed, or undeliverable.

Spam differs from other forms of direct marketing in many ways, one of them being that it costs little more to send to a larger number of recipients than a smaller number. For this reason, there is little pressure upon spammers to limit the number of addresses targeted in a spam run, or to restrict it to persons likely to be interested. One consequence of this fact is that many people receive spam written in languages they cannot read - a good deal of spam sent to English-speaking recipients is in Chinese or Korean, for instance. Likewise, lists of addresses sold for use in spam frequently contain malformed addresses, duplicate addresses, and addresses of role accounts such as postmaster.

Spammers may harvest e-mail addresses from a number of sources. A popular method uses e-mail addresses which their owners have published for other purposes. Usenet posts, especially those in archives such as Google Groups, frequently yield addresses. Simply searching the Web for pages with addresses - such as corporate staff directories - using spambots can yield thousands of addresses, most of them deliverable. Spammers have also subscribed to discussion mailing lists for the purpose of gathering the addresses of posters.

The DNS and WHOIS systems require the publication of technical contact information for all Internet domains; spammers have illegally trawled these resources for email addresses. Many spammers utilize programs called web spiders to find email addresses on web pages.

Spammer viruses may include a function which scans the victimized computer's disk drives (and possibly its network interfaces) for email addresses. These scanners discover email addresses which have never been exposed on the Web or in Whois. A victimized computer located on a shared network segment may capture email addresses from traffic addressed to its network neighbors. The harvested addresses are then returned to the spammer through the bot-net created by the virus.

A recent, controversial tactic, called "e-pending", involves the appending of e-mail addresses to direct-marketing databases. Direct marketers normally obtain lists of prospects from sources such as magazine subscriptions and customer lists. By searching the Web and other resources for e-mail addresses corresponding to the names and street addresses in their records, direct marketers can send targeted spam e-mail. However, as with most spammer "targeting", this is imprecise; users have reported, for instance, receiving solicitations to mortgage their house at a specific street address - with the address being clearly a business address including mail stop and office number.

Spammers sometimes use various means to confirm addresses as deliverable. For instance, including a Web bug in a spam message written in HTML may cause the recipient's mail client to transmit the recipient's address, or any other unique key, to the spammer's Web site. Likewise, spammers sometimes operate Web pages which purport to remove submitted addresses from spam lists. In several cases, these have been found to subscribe the entered addresses to receive more spam.

When you fill out a form it is often sold to a spammer using a web service or http post to transfer the data. This is immediate and will drop the email in various spammer databases. The revenue made from the spammer is shared with the source. For instance if you ran an online mortgage, or signed up for a loan the owner of this site is likely to make a deal with the spammer to sell the address. These are considered the best emails by spammers because they are fresh and the user just signed up for a site that does well with spam anyway.

Sometimes, if the sent spam is "bounced" or sent back to the sender by various programs that eliminate spam, or if the recipient clicks on a unsubscribe link, that may cause that email address to be marked as "valid". Most of the time this is the case, although sometimes clicking will actually unsubscribe that email.

Delivering Spam Messages

Internet users and system administrators have deployed a vast array of techniques to block, filter, or otherwise banish spam from users' mailboxes. Almost all Internet service providers forbid the use of their services to send spam or to operate spam-support services. Both commercial firms and volunteers run subscriber services dedicated to blocking or filtering spam, such as AppRiver, GFI Software, Brightmail, SpamAssassin, MailRoute, Postini, Panda, MX Logic and the various DNSBLs.

Using Webmail services

A common practice of spammers is to create accounts on free webmail services, such as Hotmail, to send spam or to receive e-mailed responses from potential customers. Because of the amount of mail sent by spammers, they require several e-mail accounts, and use web bots to automate the creation of these accounts.

In an effort to cut down on this abuse, many of these services have adopted a system called the captcha: users attempting to create a new account are presented with a graphic of a word, which uses a strange font, on a difficult to read background. Humans are able to read these graphics, and are required to enter the word to complete the application for a new account, while computers are unable to get accurate readings of the words using standard OCR techniques. Blind users of captchas typically get an audio sample.

Spammers have, however, found a means of circumventing this measure. Reportedly, they have set up sites offering free pornography: to get access to the sité, a user displays a graphic from one of these webmail sites, and must enter the word. Once the bot has successfully created the account, the user gains access to the pornographic material.

Using other people's computers

Early on, spammers discovered that if they sent large quantities of spam directly from their ISP accounts, recipients would complain and ISPs would shut their accounts down. Thus, one of the basic techniques of sending spam has become to send it from someone else's computer and network connection. By doing this, spammers protect themselves in several ways: they hide their tracks, get others' systems to do most of the work of delivering messages, and direct the efforts of investigators towards the other systems rather than the spammers themselves. The increasing broadband usage gave rise to a great number of computers that are online as long as they are turned on, and whose owners do not always take steps to protect them from malware. A botnet consisting of several hundred compromised machines can effortlessly churn out millions of messages per day. This also complicates the tracing of spammers.

Open relays: In the 1990s, the most common way spammers did this was to use open mail relays. An open relay is an MTA, or mail server, which is configured to pass along messages sent to it from any location, to any recipient. In the original SMTP mail architecture, this was the default behaviour: a user could send mail to practically any mail server, which would pass it along towards the intended recipient's mail server.

The standard was written in an era before spamming when there were few hosts on the internet, and those on the internet abided by a certain level of conduct. While this cooperative, open approach was useful in ensuring that mail was delivered, it was vulnerable to abuse by spammers. Spammers could forward batches of spam through open relays, leaving the job of delivering the messages up to the relays.

In response, mail system administrators concerned about spam began to demand that other mail operators configure MTAs to cease being open relays. The first DNSBLs, such as MAPS RBL and the now-defunct ORBS, aimed chiefly at allowing mail sites to refuse mail from known open relays.

Open proxies: Within a few years, open relays became rare and spammers resorted to other tactics, most prominently the use of open proxies. A proxy is a network service for making indirect connections to other network services. The client connects to the proxy and instructs it to connect to a server. The server perceives an incoming connection from the proxy, not the original client. Proxies have many purposes, including Web-page caching, protection of privacy, filtering of Web content, and selectively bypassing firewalls.

An open proxy is one which will create connections for any client to any server, without authentication. Like open relays, open proxies were once relatively common, as many administrators did not see a need to restrict access to them. A spammer can direct an open proxy to connect to a mail server, and send spam through it. The mail server logs a connection from the proxy — not the spammer's own computer. This provides an even greater degree of concealment for the spammer than an open relay, since most relays log the client address in the headers of messages they pass. Open proxies have also been used to conceal the sources of attacks against other services besides mail, such as Web sites or IRC servers.

Besides relays and proxies, spammers have used other insecure services to send spam. One example is FormMail.pl, a CGI script to allow Web-site users to send e-mail feedback from an HTML form. Several versions of this programme, and others like it, allowed the user to redirect e-mail to arbitrary addresses. Spam sent through open FormMail scripts is frequently marked by the program's characteristic opening line: "Below is the result of your feedback form."

As spam from proxies and other "spammable" resources grew, DNSBL operators started listing their IP addresses, as well as open relays.

MAKE MONEY FAST

"Make money fast" is a title of an electronically forwarded chain letter which became so infamous that the term is now used to describe all sorts of chain letters forwarded over the Internet, by e-mail spam or Usenet newsgroups. In anti-spammer slang, the name is often abbreviated "MMF".

The original "Make Money Fast" letter was written around 1988 by a person who used the name Dave Rhodes. Biographical details are not certain, and it is not clear that this is even the person's actual name. It is often said, such as in the FAQ for the net.legends Usenet group, that Rhodes was a student at Columbia Union College, a Christian college in Maryland, who wrote a text file chain letter titled "Make Money Fast", and uploaded it to a nearby BBS around 1987.

It is also often said that Rhodes was convicted of some fraud-related crime and that as part of his sentence he had to create an anti-spam website, but no evidence of this has been found. The scam reached the Internet, where it was forwarded over e-mail and Usenet, although it was not until spamming became a major problem in 1994 that "Make money fast" exploded. It became one of the most persistent spams in existence and multiple variations have evolved, often by spammers who change the subject of their email to "This really works!" or "You are a winner!"

Mechanics and Legality

The "Make Money Fast" chain letter encouraged readers of the email to forward one dollar in cash to a list of people provided in the text, and to add their own name and address to the bottom of the list after deleting the name and address at the top. Using the theory behind pyramid schemes, the resulting chain of money flowing back and forth would supposedly deliver a reward of thousands of dollars to the ones participating in the chain, as copies of their chain spread and more and more people sent one dollar to their address.

The text of "Make money fast" originally claimed to be "perfectly legal", citing Title 18, U.S. Code, Sections 1302 (which deals with postal lotteries) and 1341 (which deals with mail fraud). The U.S. Postal Inspection Service cites 18 USC 1302 when it asserts the illegality of chain letters, including MMF:

> Chain letters are illegal if they request money or other items of value and promise a substantial return to the participants. Chain letters are a form of gambling, and sending them through the mail (or delivering them in person or by computer, but mailing money to participate) violates Title 18, United States Code, Section 1302, the Postal Lottery Statute.

It also asserts that "[r]egardless of what technology is used to advance the scheme, if the mail is used at any step along the way, it is still illegal." The U.S. Postal Inspection Service asserts the mathematical impossibility that all participants will be winners, as well as the possibilities that:

— participants may fail to send money to the first person listed, and

— the perpetrator may have listed himself multiple times under different addresses and names, thus ensuring that all the money go to the same person.

Anti-spam Techniques (e-mail)

To prevent e-mail spam, both end users and administrators of e-mail systems use various anti-spam techniques. Some of these techniques have been embedded in products, services and software to ease the burden on users and administrators. No one technique is a complete solution to the spam problem, and each has trade-offs between incorrectly rejecting legitimate e-mail vs. not rejecting all spam, and the associated costs in time and effort.

Anti-spam techniques can be broken into four broad categories: those that require actions by individuals, those that can be automated by the email administrator, those that can be automated by e-mail senders and those employed by researchers and law enforcement officials.

End-user techniques

There are a number of techniques that individuals can use to restrict the availability of their e-mail addresses, reducing or preventing their attractiveness to spam.

Address munging

Posting anonymously, or with a fake name and address, is one way to avoid "address harvesting," but users should ensure that the fake address is not valid. Users who want to receive legitimate email regarding their posts or Web sites can alter their addresses so humans can figure out but spammers cannot. For instance, joe@example.net might post as joeNOS@PAM.example.net.invalid, or display his email address as an image instead of text. Address munging, however, can cause legitimate replies to be lost. And if it's not the user's valid address, it has to be truly invalid, otherwise someone or some server will still get the spam for it.

Avoid responding

Spammers often regard responses to their messages-even responses like "Don't spam me"-as confirmation that an email address is valid. Likewise, many spam messages contain Web links or addresses which the user is directed to follow to be removed from the spammer's mailing list. In several cases, spam-fighters have tested these links, confirming they do not lead to the recipient address's removal-if anything, they lead to more spam.

It must be noted that sender addresses are often forged in spam messages, so that responding to spam may result in failed deliveries or may reach innocent e-mail users whose addresses have been abused. In many countries providing a false identity in that way is a criminal offense. Criminal spammers sometimes send their messages from purposely compromised computers in order to hide their real identity. Benign spammers reveal their identity, allowing recipients to respond.

In Usenet, it is widely considered even more important to avoid responding to spam. Many ISPs have software that seek and destroy duplicate messages. Someone may see a spam and respond to it before it is cancelled by their server, which can have the effect of reposting the spam for them; since it is not a duplicate, the reposted copy will last longer.

Contact forms

Contact forms allow users to send email by filling out forms in a web browser. The web server takes the form data, forwarding it to an email address. The user never sees the email address. Contact forms have the drawback that they require a website that supports server side scripts. They are also inconvenient to the message sender as they are not able to use their preferred e-mail client. Finally if the software used to run the contact forms is badly designed they can become spam tools in their own right. Additionally many spammers have taken to using contact forms to send spam to the intended recipient.

Disable HTML in e-mail

Many modern mail programs incorporate Web browser functionality, such as the display of HTML, URLs, and images. This can easily expose the user to offensive images in spam. In addition, spam written in HTML can contain web bugs which allows spammers to see that the e-mail address is valid and that the message has not been caught in spam filters. JavaScript programs can be used to direct the user's Web browser to an advertised page, or to make the spam message difficult to close or delete. Spam messages have contained attacks upon security vulnerabilities in the HTML renderer, using these holes to install spyware.

Mail clients which do not automatically download and display HTML, images or attachments, have fewer risks, as do clients have been configured to not display these by default.

Disposable e-mail addresses

Many email users sometimes need to give an address to a site without complete assurance that the site will not send out spam. One way to mitigate the risk is to provide a disposable email address-a temporary address which forwards email to a real account, which the user can disable or abandon. A number of services provide disposable address forwarding. Addresses can be manually disabled, can expire after a given time interval, or can expire after a certain number of messages have been forwarded.

Reporting spam

Tracking down a spammer's ISP and reporting the offense can lead to the spammer's service being terminated. Unfortunately, it can be difficult to track down the spammer-and while there are some online tools to assist, they are not always accurate. Occasionally, spammers employ their own netblocks. In this case, the abuse contact for the netblock can be the spammer itself and can confirm your address.

Examples of these online tools are SpamCop and Network Abuse Clearinghouse. They provide automated or semi-automated means to report spam to ISPs. Some spam-fighters regard them as inaccurate compared to what an expert in the email system can do; however, most email users are not experts.

A useful free tool that may be used in the reporting of spam is also available (Complainterator). The Complainterator will send an automatically-generated complaint to the registrar of the spamming domain and the registrar of its name servers. Historically, reporting spam in this way has not seriously abated spam, since the spammers simply move their operation to another url, ISP or network of IP addresses.

Consumers may also forward "unwanted or deceptive spam" to an email address maintained by the FTC. The database collected is used to prosecute perpetrators of scam or deceptive advertising. An alternative to contacting ISPs is to contact the registrar of a domain name that has used in spam e-mail. Registrars, as ICANN-accredited administrative organizations, are obliged to uphold certain rules and regulations, and have the resources necessary for dealing with abuse complaints.

Responding to spam

Some advocate responding aggressively to spam-in other words, "spamming the spammer". The basic idea is to make spamming less attractive to the spammer, by increasing the spammer's overhead. There are several ways to reach a spammer, but besides the caveats above, it may lead to retaliations by the spammer.

— Replying directly to the spammer's email address. Just clicking "reply" will not work in the vast majority of cases, since most of the sender addresses are forged or made up. In some cases, however, spammers do provide valid addresses, as in the case of Nigerian scams.

— Targeting the computers used to send out spam. In 2005, IBM announced a service to bounce spam directly to the computers that send out spam. Because the IP addresses are identified in the headers of every message, it would be possible to target those computers directly, sidestepping the problem of forged email addresses. In most cases, however, those computers do not belong to the real spammer, but to unsuspecting users with unsecured or outdated systems, hijacked through malware and controlled at distance by the spammer.

— Leaving messages on the spamvertised site. Spammers selling their wares need a tangible point of contact so that customers can reach them. Sometimes it is a telephone number, but most often is a web site containing web forms through which customers can fill out orders or inquiries, or even "unsubscribe" requests. Since positive response to spam is probably much less than 1/10,000, if just a tiny percentage of users visit spam sites just to leave negative messages, the negative messages could easily outnumber positive ones, incurring costs for spammers to sort them out, not mentioning the cost in bandwidth. This was the approach used by the now-defunct Blue Security's Blue Frog service: it looked for web forms on those sites and filled one form on behalf of the subscriber for each spam received, thus overwhelming spammer sites (Blue Frog service had up to a half million users). Ironically, it was Blue Frog's effectiveness that brought it down, by attracting a massive, retaliatory denial-of-service attack from a spammer who refused to fold. After the demise of Blue Frog, other services have been trying to replicate its ideas, while avoiding its shortcomings.

Automated Techniques

There are a number of appliances, services and software systems that e-mail administrators can use to reduce the load of spam on their systems and mailboxes. Some of these depend upon rejecting email from Internet sites known or likely to send spam. Others rely on automatically analyzing the content of email messages and weeding out those which resemble spam. These two approaches are sometimes termed blocking and filtering.

There is an increasing trend of integration of anti-spam techniques into MTAs whereby the mail systems themselves also perform various measures that are generally referred to as filtering, ultimately resulting in spams being rejected before delivery (or blocked).

Many filtering systems take advantage of machine learning techniques, which improve their accuracy over manual methods. However, some people find filtering intrusive to privacy, and many e-mail administrators prefer blocking to deny access to their systems from sites tolerant of spammers.

Authentication

A number of systems have been proposed to allow acceptance of email from servers which have authenticated in some fashion as senders of only legitimate email. Many of these systems use the DNS, as do DNSBLs; but rather than being used to list nonconformant sites, the DNS is used to list sites authorized to send email, and (sometimes) to determine the reputation of those sites. Other methods of identifying ham and spam are still used.

Authentication systems cannot detect whether a message is spam. Rather, they allow a site to express trust that an authenticated site will not send spam. Thus, a recipient site may choose to skip expensive spam-filtering methods for messages from authenticated sites.

Challenge-response spam filtering

Another method which may be used by internet service providers, by specialized services or enterprises to combat spam is to require unknown senders to pass various tests before their messages are delivered. These strategies are termed challenge/response systems or C/R. Some view their use as being as bad as spam since they place the burden of spam fighting on legitimate email senders.

Checksum-based filtering

Checksum-based filter exploits the fact that the messages are sent in bulk, that is that they will be identical with small variations. Checksum-based filters strip out everything that might vary between messages, reduce what remains to a checksum, and look that checksum up in a database which collects the checksums of messages that email recipients consider to be spam ; if the checksum is in the database, the message is likely to be spam.

The advantage of this type of filtering is that it lets ordinary users help identify spam, and not just administrators, thus vastly increasing the pool of spam fighters. The disadvantage is that spammers can insert unique invisible gibberish-known as hashbusters-into the middle of each of their messages, thus making each message unique and having a different checksum. This leads to an arms race between the developers of the checksum software and the developers of the spam-generating software.

Checksum based filtering methods include:

— Distributed Checksum Clearinghouse

— Vipul's Razor

— Recurrent Pattern Detection

Country-based filtering

Some e-mail servers expect to never communicate with particular countries from which they receive a great deal of spam. Therefore, they use country-based filtering - a technique that blocks e-mail from certain countries. This technique is based on country of origin determined by the sender's IP address rather than any trait of the sender.

DNSBLs

DNS-based Blackhole Lists, or DNSBLs, are used fo heuristic filtering and blocking. A site publishes list (typically of IP addresses) via the DNS, in such a wa that mail servers can easily be set to reject mail from thos sources. There are literally scores of DNSBLs, each which reflects different policies: some list sites known emit spam; others list open mail relays or proxies; oth list ISPs known to support spam. Other DNS-based ar spam systems list known good ("white") or bad ("blac IPs domains or URLs, including RHSBLs and URIBLs. history, details, and examples of DNSBLs, see DNSBI

Enforcing RFC standards

Enforcing technical requirements of the Simple Mail Transfer Protocol (SMTP) can be used to block mail coming from systems that do not comply with the RFC standards. A lot of spammers use poorly written software or are unable to comply with the standards because they do not have legitimate control of the computer sending spam (zombie computer). By setting restrictions on the MTA a mail administrator can reduce spam significantly.

HELO/EHLO checking: For example, spam can be greatly reduced by a number of simple checks confirming compliance with standard addressing and MTA operation. In many situations, simply requiring a valid FQDN in the SMTP EHLO statement is enough to block 25% of incoming spam.

— Refusing connections from hosts that begin transmission prior to presentation of the receiving host's HELO banner

— Refusing connections from hosts that give an invalid HELO - for example, a HELO that is not an FQDN or is an IP address not surrounded by square brackets

— Refusing connections from hosts that give an obviously fraudulent HELO - for example, issuing a HELO using the FQDN or an IP address that doesn't match the IP address of the connecting host

— Refusing to accept email claiming to be from a hosted domain when the sending host has not authenticated

— Refusing to accept email whose HELO/EHLO argument does not resolve in DNS. Unfortunately, some email system administrators ignore section 3.6 of RFC2821 and administer the MTA to use a nonresolvable argument to the HELO/EHLO command.

All of the examples above are fairly simple checks, all conform to existing standards and RFCs, and all are missing from most commercial MTA implementations available today.

Greylisting: The SMTP allows for temporary rejection of incoming messages. Greylisting is the technique to temporarily reject messages from unknown sender mail servers. A temporary rejection is designated with a 4xx error code that is recognized by all normal MTAs, which then proceed to retry delivery later.

Greylisting is based on the premise that spammers and spambots will not re-try their messages. Instead, they will move on to the next message and next address. This is effective since a re-try attempt means the message and state of the process must be stored inherently increasing the cost incurred by the spammer, but a standard component of any legitimate sender's server.

Fake MX Records

Virus infected spam bots ignore requirements that the email start at the lowest numbered MX record and move up the list if a failure occurs. They try the highest numbered MX records first thinking that the backup servers have less spam filtering than the low numbered MX servers. Spam bots usually do not retry on failure but move on to the next email address in their list. Thus adding fake high numbered MX records is an effective way to reduce incoming spam.

One can also reduce spam but having a fake lowest MX record as well. This causes real email to have to retry as well but it only adds a second to the delivery time. Some people report as much as 90% reduction in spam bot spam using this method.

Greeting delay

A greeting delay is a deliberate pause introduced by an SMTP server before it sends the SMTP greeting banner to the client. The client is supposed to wait until it has received this banner before it sends any data to the server. Many spam-sending applications do not wait to receive this banner, and instead start sending data once the TCP connection is complete. The server can detect this, and drop the connection.

There are some legitimate sites that play "fast and loose" with the SMTP specifications, and may be caught by this mechanism. It also has a tendency to interact badly with sites that perform Callback Verification, as common callback verification systems have timeouts that are much shorter than those mandated by RFC2821 4.5.3.2.

Hybrid filtering

Hybrid filtering, such as is implemented in the open source programs SpamAssassin and Policyd-weight, uses some or all of the various tests for spam, and assigns a numerical score to each test. Each message is scanned for these patterns, and the applicable scores tallied up. If the total is above a fixed value, the message is rejected or flagged as spam. By ensuring that no single spam test by itself can flag a message as spam, the false positive rate can be greatly reduced.

PTR/Reverse DNS checks

The PTR DNS records in the reverse DNS can be used for a number of things, including:

— Most e-mail Mail Transfer Agents (server software) use a FCrDNS verification and if there is a valid domain name, put it into the "Received:" trace header field.

— Some e-mail Mail Transfer Agents will perform FCrDNS verification on the domain name given on the SMTP HELO and EHLO commands. This can violate RFC 2821 and so e-mail is usually not rejected by default.

— To check the domain names in the rDNS to see if they are likely from dial-up users, dynamically assigned addresses, or home-based broadband customers. Since the vast majority, but by no means all, of e-mail that originates from these computers is spam, many mail servers also refuse e-mail with missing or "generic" rDNS names.

— A Forward Confirmed reverse DNS (FCrDNS) verification can create a weak form of authentication that there is a valid relationship between the owner of a domain name and the owner of the network that has been given an IP address. While weak, this authentication is strong enough that it can be used for whitelisting purposes because spammers and phishers cannot usually bypass this verification when they use zombie computers to forge the domains.

Rule-based filtering

Content filtering techniques relied on the specification of lists of words or regular expressions disallowed in mail messages. Thus, if a site receives spam advertising "herbal Viagra", the administrator might place these words in the filter configuration. The mail server would thence reject any message containing the phrase.

Header filtering is the means of inspecting the header of the email, the part of the message that contains information about the message. Spammers will often spoof fields in the header in order to hide their identities, or to try to make the email look more legitimate than it is; many of these spoofing methods can be detected. Also, headers that violate the RFC 2822 standard on how the email header is to be formed are frequently rejected.

Disadvantages of filtering are threefold: First, it can be time-consuming to maintain. Second, it is prone to false positives. Third, these false positives are not equally distributed: since content filtering is prone to reject legitimate messages on topics related to products frequently advertised in spam. A system administrator who attempts to reject spam messages which advertise mortgage refinancing, credit or debt may inadvertently block legitimate e-mail on the same subject.

Spammers frequently change the phrases and spellings they use. This can mean more work for the administrator. However, it also has some advantages for the spam fighter. If the spammer starts spelling "Viagra" as "V1agra" or "Via_gra", it makes it harder for the spammer's intended audience to read their messages. If they try to trip up the phrase detector, by, for example, inserting an invisible-to-the-user HTML comment in the middle of a word ("Via<!——>gra"), this sleight of hand is itself easily detectable, and is a good indication that the message is spam. And if they send spam that consists entirely of images, so that anti-spam software can't analyze the words and phrases in the message, the fact that there is no readable text in the body can be detected, making that message a higher risk of being spam.

Content filtering can also be implemented to examine the URLs present (i.e. spamvertising) in an email message. This form of content filtering is much harder to disguise as the URLs must resolve to a valid domain name. Extracting a list of such links and comparing them to published sources of spamvertised domains is a simple and reliable way to eliminate a large percentage of spam via content analysis.

Sender-supported whitelists and tags

There are a small number of organizations which offer IP whitelisting and/or licensed tags that can be placed in email (for a fee) to assure recipients' systems that the messages thus tagged are not spam. This system relies on legal enforcement of the tag. The intent is for email administrators to whitelist messages bearing the licensed tag.

— Habeas Safelist

— Return Path Sender Score Certified.

A potential difficulty with such systems is that the licensing organization makes its money by licensing more senders to use the tag-not by strictly enforcing the rules upon licensees. A concern exists that senders whose messages are more likely to be considered spam who would accrue a greater benefit by using such a tag. The concern is that these factors form a perverse incentive for licensing organizations to be lenient with licensees who have offended. However, the value of a license would drop if it was not strictly enforced, and financial gains due to enforcement of a license itself can provide an additional incentive for strict enforcement. The Habeas mail classing system attempts to further address this issue by classing email according to origin, purpose, and permission. The purpose is to describe why the email is not likely spam, but permission based email.

Callback verification

Since a large percentage of spam has forged and invalid sender ("from") addresses, some spam can be detected by checking that this "from" address is valid. A mail server can try to verify the sender address by making an SMTP connection back to the mail exchanger for the address, as if it was creating a bounce, but stopping just before any e-mail is sent.

Callback verification can be compliant with SMTP RFCs, but it has various drawbacks. Since nearly all spam has forged return addresses, nearly all callbacks are to innocent third party mail servers that are unrelated to the spam. At the same time, there will be numerous false negatives due to spammers abusing real addresses and some false positives.

Statistical content filtering

Statistical filtering was first proposed in 1998 by Mehran Sahami et al., at the AAAI-98 Workshop on Learning for Text Categorization. A statistical filter is a kind of document classification system, and a number of machine learning researchers have turned their attention to the problem. Statistical filtering was popularized by Paul Graham's influential 2002 article A Plan for Spam, which proposed the use of naive Bayes classifiers to predict whether messages are spam or not - based on collections of spam and nonspam ("ham") email submitted by users.

Statistical filtering, once set up, requires no maintenance per se: instead, users mark messages as spam or nonspam and the filtering software learns from these judgements. Thus, a statistical filter does not reflect the software author's or administrator's biases as to content, but it does reflect the user's biases as to content; a biochemist who is researching Viagra won't have messages containing the word "Viagra" flagged as spam, because "Viagra" will show up often in his or her legitimate messages. Spam emails containing the word "Viagra", however, do get filtered because of their unique content compared to legitimate messages. A statistical filter can also respond quickly to changes in spam content, without administrative intervention. Statistical filters should also look at message headers , thereby considering not just the content but also peculiarities of the transport mechanism of the email.

Spammers have attempted to fight statistical filtering by inserting many random but valid "noise" words or sentences into their messages while attempting to hide them from view, making it more likely that the filter will classify the message as neutral. (See Word salad (computer science).) Attempts to hide the noise words include setting them in tiny font or the same colour as the background. However, these noise countermeasures seem to have been largely ineffective.

Software programs that implement statistical filtering include Bogofilter, DSPAM, SpamBayes the e-mail programs Mozilla and Mozilla Thunderbird, Mailwasher, and later revisions of SpamAssassin. Another interesting project is CRM114 which hashes phrases and does bayesian classification on the phrases. There is also the free mail filter POPFile which sorts mail in as many categories as you want (family, friends, co-worker, spam, whatever) with bayesian filtering.

Tarpits

A tarpit is any server software which intentionally responds pathologically slowly to client commands. This is not to be confused with slow speeds sometimes experienced by Telecoms clients (or most of the time if using the South African Telecoms monopoly). By running a tarpit which treats acceptable mail normally and known spam slowly or which appears to be an open mail relay, a site can slow down the rate at which spammers can inject messages into the mail facility. Many systems will simply disconnect if the server doesn't respond quickly, which will eliminate the spam. However, a few legitimate e-mail systems will also not deal correctly with these delays.

Transparent SMTP proxy

Transparent SMTP proxies allow combating spam in real time, combining sender's behaviour controls, providing legitimate users immediate feedback, eliminating a need for quarantine.

X-ASVP eXtensible Anti-spam Verification Protocol

X-ASVP is an paper design of a method to enable peer to peer scalable authentication between holders of an Internet e-mail address, with redundancy and reliability provided by secondary (tld) and tertiary (global) providers. Its proponents claim that a prototype implementation exists.

Automated Techniques

There are a variety of techniques that e-mail senders use to try to make sure that they do not send spam. Failure to control the amount of spam sent, as judge by e-mail receivers, can often cause even legitimate email to be blocked and for the sender to be put on DNSBLs.

Since spammers are frequently kicked off the network, they are constantly trying to create new accounts. Many spammers are able to make even a few hours profitable for them and can cause many days of damage to reputation of the services they abused. As a result, many ISPs and web -email providers use CAPTCHAs on new accounts and try to verify the credit cards are not stolen before accepting new customers, check the Spamhaus Project ROKSO list and do other background checks.

Opt in e-mail

One difficulty occurs in implementing opt-in mailing lists: many means of gathering user e-mail addresses remain susceptible to forgery. For instance, if a company puts up a Web form to allow users to subscribe to a mailing list about its products, a malicious person can enter other people's e-mail addresses - to harass them, or to make the company appear to be spamming.

To prevent this abuse, MAPS and other anti-spam organizations encourage that all mailing lists use confirmed opt-in (also known as verified opt-in and (by spammers themselves) as double opt-in). That is, whenever an address is presented for subscription to the list, the list software should send a confirmation message to that address. The confirmation message contains no advertising content, so it is not construed to be spam itself - and the address is not added to the list unless the recipient responds to the confirmation message. See also the Spamhaus Mailing Lists vs. Spam Lists page.

All modern mailing list management programs (such as GNU Mailman, Majordomo, and qmail's ezmlm) support confirmed opt-in by default.

Egress filtering

E-mail senders can do the same type of anti-spam checks e-mail coming from their users and customers as can be done for e-mail coming from the rest of the Internet.

Limit e-mail backscatter

If any sort of bounce message or antivirus warning gets sent to a forged email address, the result will be e-mail backscatter. Problems with sending challenges to forged e-mail addresses can be greatly reduced by not creating a new message that contains the challenge. Instead, the challenge can be placed in the Bounce message when the receiving mail system gives a rejection-code during the SMTP session. When the receiving mail system rejects an e-mail this way, it is the sending system that actually creates the bounce message. As a result, the bounce message will almost always be sent to the real sender, and it will be in a format and language that the sender will usually recognize.

Port 25 blocking

Firewalls and routers can be programmed to not allow SMTP traffic (TCP port 25) from machines that are not supposed to run Mail Transfer Agents or send e-mail. This practice is somewhat controversial when ISPs block home users, especially if the ISPs do not allow the blocking to be turned off upon request. E-mail can still be sent from these computers to designated smart hosts via port 25 and to other smart hosts via the e-mail submission port 587.

Port 25 interception

Network address translation can be used intercept all port 25 (SMTP) traffic and direct it to a mail server that enforces rate limiting and egress spam filtering. This is commonly done in hotels, but it can cause e-mail privacy problems, as well making it impossible to use STARTTLS and SMTP-AUTH if the port 587 submission port isn't used.

Rate limiting

Machines that suddenly start sending lots of e-mail may well have become zombie computers. By limiting the rate that e-mail can be sent around what is typical for the computer in question, legitimate e-mail can still be sent, but large spam runs can be slowed down until manual investigation can be done.

Feedback loops

By monitoring spam reports from places such as spamcop, AOL's feedback loop, and Network Abuse Clearinghouse, the domains abuse@ mailbox, etc., ISPs can often learn of problems before they seriously damage the ISP's reputation and have their mail servers blacklisted.

Strong AUP

Most ISPs and web e-mail providers have either an Acceptable use policy (AUP) or a Terms of Service (TOS) agreement that discourages spammers from using their system and allows the spammer to be terminated quickly.

Techniques for researchers

Increasingly, anti-spam efforts have required co-ordination between law enforcement, researchers, major consumer financial service companies and Internet service providers who need e-mail spam, identity theft and phishing evidence to track and monitor the risks and activities.

Honeypots

Another approach is simply an imitation MTA which gives the appearance of being an open mail relay, or an imitation TCP/IP proxy server which gives the appearance of being an open proxy. Spammers who probe systems for open relays/proxies will find such a host and attempt to send mail through it, wasting their time and potentially revealing information about themselves and the source of spam to the unexpected alert entity (in comparison to the anticipated careless or unskilled operator typically in charge of open relay MTA systems) that operates the honeypot. Such a system may simply discard the spam attempts, submit them to DNSBLs, or store them for analysis.

Ongoing Research

Several approaches have been proposed to improve the e-mail system.

Ham passwords

Another approach for countering spam is to use a "ham password". Systems that use ham passwords ask unrecognised senders to include in their email a password that demonstrates that the email message is a "ham" (not spam) message. Typically the email address and ham password would be described on a web page, and the ham password would be included in the "subject" line of an email address. Ham passwords are often combined with filtering systems, to counter the risk that a filtering system will accidentally identify a ham message as a spam message. The "plus addressing" technique appends a password to the "username" part of the email address.

Cost-based systems

Since spam occurs primarily because it is so cheap to send, a proposed set of solutions require that senders pay some cost in order to send spam, making it prohibitively expensive for spammers.

Stamps: Some gatekeeper would sell electronic stamps and keep the proceeds. Or a micropayment, such as electronic money would be paid by the sender to the recipient or their ISP, or some other gatekeeper.

Proof-of-work systems: Proof-of-work systems such as hashcash require that a sender pay a computational cost by performing a calculation that the receiver can later verify. Verification must be much faster than performing the calculation, so that the computation slows down a sender but does not significantly impact a receiver. The point is to slow down machines that send most of spam-often millions and millions of them. While every user that wants to send email to a moderate number of recipients suffers just a few seconds' delay, sending millions of emails would take an unaffordable amount of time. This approach suffers when sender maintains a computation farm of their own or from zombies.

Sender-at-risk: As a refinement to stamp systems was the idea of requiring that the micropayment only be retained if the recipient considered the email to be abusive. This addressed the principal objection to stamp systems: popular free legitimate mailing list hosts would be unable to continue to provide their services if they had to pay postage for every message they sent out.

Bill Gates announced that Microsoft is working on a solution requiring so-called "unknown senders", i.e. senders not on the Accepted List of the recipient to post "the electronic equivalent of a" stamp whose value would be lost to the sender only if the recipient disapproves of the email . Gates said that Microsoft favors other solutions in the short-term, but would rely on the contingent payment solution to solve the spam problem over the longer run. Microsoft, AOL as well as Yahoo! have recently introduced systems that allow commercial senders to avoid filters if they obtain a certificate or certification, which is lost to the sender if recipients complain.

The intent of such "sender-at-risk" solutions, which impose a significant cost to the sender only if the recipient rejects the message subsequent to receiving the email, is to deter spam by making it economically prohibitive to send unwanted email messages, while allowing legitimate emailers to send messages at little or no expense.

SHRED: Spam Harassment Reduction via Economic Disincentives (SHRED) is a recent proposal for a sender-at-risk protocol that aims to avoid some of the defects of earlier reputation and postage-based systems.

Spamming

Spamming is the abuse of electronic messaging systems

to indiscriminately send unsolicited bulk messages. While the most widely recognized form of spam is e-mail spam, the term is applied to similar abuses in other media: instant messaging spam, Usenet news group spam, Web search engine spam, spam in blogs, mobile phone messaging spam, internet forum spam and junk fax transmissions.

Spamming is economically viable because advertisers have no operating costs beyond the management of their mailing lists, and it is difficult to hold senders accountable for their mass mailings. Because the barrier to entry is so low, spammers are numerous, and the volume of unsolicited mail has become very high. The costs, such as lost productivity and fraud, are borne by the public and by Internet service providers, which have been forced to add extra capacity to cope with the deluge. Spamming is widely reviled, and has been the subject of legislation in many jurisdictions.

Spamming in different media

Instant Messaging spam, sometimes termed spim (a portmanteau of spam and IM, short for instant messenger), makes use of instant messaging systems, such as AOL Instant Messenger, ICQ or Windows Live Messenger. Many IM systems offer a user directory, including demographic information that allows an advertiser to gather the information, sign on to the system, and send unsolicited messages. To send instant messages to millions of users requires scriptable software and the recipients' IM usernames. Spammers have similarly targeted Internet Relay Chat channels, using IRC bots that join channels and bombard them with advertising.

Messenger service spam has lent itself to spammer use in a particularly circular scheme. In many cases, messenger spammers send messages to vulnerable machines consisting of text like "Annoyed by these messages? Visit this site." The link leads to a Web site where, for a fee, users are told how to disable the Windows messenger service. Though the messenger service is easily disabled for free, the scam works because it creates a perceived need and offers a solution. Often the only "annoying messages" the user receives through Messenger are ads to disable Messenger itself. It is often using a false ID to get money or credit card numbers.

Chat spam

Chat spam can occur in any live chat environment like IRC and in-game multiplayer chat of online games. It consists of repeating the same word or sentence many times to get attention or to interfere with normal operations. It is generally considered very rude and may lead to swift exclusion of the user from the used chat service by the owners or moderators.

The application of the name "Spam" to unwanted communication originates in Chat-room spam. Specifically, it was developed in the chat-rooms of People-Link in the early 1980s as a technique for getting rid of unwelcome newcomers. When someone would enter a chat-room full of friends who were in mid-conversation, and when the newcomer tried to turn the conversation in an unwelcome direction, two veteran members of the room would begin typing in the Monty Python "Spam" routine at high speed. They would fill the screen with "Spam Spam Spam eggs Spam Spam and Spam" etc, and make all other communication impossible. The other members of the room would just wait quietly until the newcomer got disgusted and moved on to a different room.

Mobile phone spam

Mobile phone spam is directed at the text messaging

service of a mobile phone. This can be especially irritating to customers not only for the inconvenience but also because of the fee they may be charged per text message received in some markets. The term "SpaSMS" was coined at the adnews website Adland in 2000 to describe spam SMS.

Online game messaging spam

Many online games allow players to contact each other via player-to-player messaging, chatrooms, or public discussion areas. What qualifies as spam varies from game to game, but usually this term applies to all forms of message flooding, violating the terms of service contract for the website.

Spamdexing

Spamdexing (a portmanteau of spamming and indexing) refers to the practice on the World Wide Web of modifying HTML pages to increase the chances of them being placed high on search engine relevancy lists. These sites use "black hat search engine optimization techniques" to unfairly increase their rank in search engines. Many modern search engines modified their search algorithms to try to exclude web pages utilizing spamdexing tactics.

Blog, wiki, and guestbook spam

Blog spam, or "blam" for short, is spamming on weblogs. In 2003, this type of spam took advantage of the open nature of comments in the blogging software Movable Type by repeatedly placing comments to various blog posts that provided nothing more than a link to the spammer's commercial web site. Similar attacks are often performed against wikis and guestbooks, both of which accept user contributions.

Spam targeting video sharing sites

Video sharing sites, such as YouTube, are now being frequently targeted by spammers. The most common technique involves people (or spambots) posting links to sites, most likely pornographic or dealing with online dating, on the comments section of random videos or people's profiles.

Another frequently used technique is using bots to post messages on random users' profiles to a spam account's channel page, along with enticing text and images, usually of a suggestive nature. These pages may include their own or other users' videos, again often suggestive. The main purpose of these accounts is to draw people to their link in the "home page" section of their profile.

YouTube has blocked the posting of links but people can still manage to get their message across by replacing with "dot"; for instance, example dot com instead of example.com. In addition, YouTube has implemented a CAPTCHA system that makes rapid posting of repeated comments much more difficult than before, due to abuse in the past by mass-spammers.

Another form of such spam is posting a message which claims to elicit an occurrence, such as an easter egg, the loss of a loved one, or being haunted by a ghost, unless a demand is met, mostly copying and pasting the message to post a certain number of times within a time limit. Such a post targets the gullible, but those who see past usually respond with derision. Some sites have a feature which marks a post as spam or a rating which blocks unwanted comments.

Noncommercial spam

E-mail and other forms of spamming have been used for

purposes other than advertisements. Many early Usenet spams were religious or political. Serdar Argic, for instance, spammed Usenet with historical revisionist screeds. A number of evangelists have spammed Usenet and e-mail media with preaching messages. A growing number of criminals are also using spam to perpetrate various sorts of fraud, and in some cases have used it to lure people to locations where they have been kidnapped, held for ransom, and even murdered.

Hobbit spam

In early July 2006 there was an enormous increase in unsolicited messages from a spoofed address with approximately half a dozen random letter subjects, containing nothing but three lines from JRR Tolkien's The Hobbit. This follows fairly closely another similar form dubbed "discordian poetry" that appeared to use a random word generator of the same. The messages had no attempt to sell anything; it was theorised that this was a script kiddie ineptly running a spam suite. This was confirmed when shortly afterward the same format messages began appearing with image files overlaying the text (a common spam technique). It is suspected to be a variation from the same source and image overlays will begin appearing.

Spam as denial of service

Spamming has also been used as a denial of service ("DoS") tactic, particularly on Usenet. By overwhelming the readers of a news group with an inordinate number of nonsense messages, legitimate messages and computing resources can be lost in the deluge. Since these messages are usually forged (that is, sent falsely under regular posters' names) this tactic has come to be known as sporgery (from spam + forgery). This tactic has for instance been used by members of the Church of Scientology against the alt.religion.scientology news group and by spammers against news.admin.net-abuse.email, a forum for mail administrators to discuss spam problems. Applied to e-mail, this is termed mailbombing.

The Usenet Meow Wars (around 1996) were DoS attacks on various newsgroups aimed at specific posters that disrupted the newsgroups where they were active. The DoS attacks launched by Hipcrime, which continue today, are more crafted as DoS attacks on entire newsgroups. The alt.sex newsgroups were rendered uninhabitable by commercial porn site spammers, partially for advertising purposes and partially to destroy a perceived free competitor.

Forged e-mail spam has been used as a tool of harassment. The spammer collects a list of addresses, then sends a spam to them signed with the name of the person he or she wishes to harass. Some recipients, angry they received spam and seeing an obvious "source", will respond angrily or pursue revenge against the apparent spammer, the forgery victim. A widely known victim of this sort of harassment was Joe's CyberPost, which has lent its name to the offense: it is known as a joe job. "Joe jobs" have been used against antispammers: in recent examples, Steve Linford of Spamhaus Project and Timothy Walton, a California attorney, have been targeted. Sometimes victims (such as ROKSO-listed spammers) are subscribed to lists that don't practice verified opt-in, such as magazine subscriptions and e-mail newsletters, a practise known as subscriptionbombing.

Spammers have abused resources set up for the purposes of anonymous speech online, such as anonymous remailers. Many of these resources have been shut down, denying their services to legitimate users.

E-mail worms or viruses may be spammed to set up an initial pool of infected machines, which resend the virus to other machines in a spam-like manner. The infected machines can often be used as remote-controlled zombie computers, for more spamming or DDoS attacks. trojans are spammed to phish for bank account details, or to set up a pool of zombies without using a virus.

In gaming

In gaming, spamming is often used to describe repetitive and disruptive behaviour. In first person shooter type games, spamming refers to tactics where a player repeatedly and randomly fires into an area in the hope of scoring chance hits. Many games attempt to limit this by providing scenarios such as Capture the Flag. Spamming also describes players who repeatedly use a particular move to gain benefits over other players. This is often seen in PvP combat as well as MMORPG games.

The term also refers to the flooding of the in-game chat with frequent messaging, this is similar to messaging spam mentioned above.

14

E-mail Tracking

E-mail tracking is a method for monitoring your e-mail delivery to your intended recipient. Most tracking technologies utilize some form of digitally time-stamped record to reveal the exact time and date that your e-mail was received or opened, as well the IP address of the recipient.

E-mail tracking is useful when the sender wants to know if the intended recipient actually received the e-mail, or if they clicked the links. However, due to the nature of the technology, e-mail tracking cannot be considered an absolutely accurate indicator that a message was opened or read by the recipient. Most e-mail marketing software provides tracking features, sometimes in aggregate, and sometimes on an individual basis.

Read-Receipt Tracking

Some e-mail applications, such as Microsoft Office Outlook, employ a read-receipt tracking mechanism. The sender selects the receipt request option prior to sending the message, and then upon sending, each recipient has the option of notifying the sender that the message was received and/or read by the recipient.

However, just because you request a receipt, does not mean you will get one in return. Not all e-mail applications support the read receipt option, meaning your recipient may never be asked to provide one. In addition, recipients have the option to block each or all read request confirmations from being sent. Another potential problem with read receipts is they interrupt (and potentially annoy) your recipient, forcing them to click a notification button before they can move on with their work. So, even though it is an opt-in process, many recipients may consider it inconvenient, discourteous, or invasive, and many will decline the receipt.

Read receipts are sent back to your Inbox as e-mail messages. Additional technical information, such as who it is from, the e-mail software they use, and the IP address of the e-mail server is available inside the Internet headers of the read receipt.

E-mail Marketing

Some e-mail marketing tools include tracking as a feature. Such e-mail tracking is usually accomplished using standard web tracking devices known as cookies and web beacons. When you send a tracked e-mail message, whether it's a simple text message or a graphical html message, the e-mail marketing system may embed a tiny, invisible tracking image (a single-pixel gif, sometimes called a web beacon) within the content of the message. When the recipient opens the message, the tracking image is referenced.

When they click a link or open an attachment, another tracking code is activated. In each case a separate tracking event is recorded by the system. These response events accumulate over time in a database, enabled the e-mail marketing software to report metrics such as open-rate and click-through rates.

Privacy Issues

E-mail tracking is used by individuals, e-mail marketers, spammers and phishers, to verify that e-mails are actually read by recipients, that email addresses are valid, and that the content of e-mails has made it past spam filters. It can sometimes reveal if e-mails get forwarded (but not usually to whom). Some companies use it at the aggregate level to help determine the effectiveness of their sales and marketing messages. Other companies use it at the individual level to better understand a customer's specific areas of interest. Many people use it to detect unauthorised forwarding and distribution of their copyrighted works and emails.

When used effectively, it helps the company provide more timely, and more relevant information to the recipient. When used maliciously, it can be used to collect confidential information about businesses and individuals and to create more effective phishing schemes.

The tracking mechanisms employed are typically first-party cookies and web bugs. If you are using e-mail tracking or e-mail marketing software, your company's privacy policy should state that you may utilise tracking devices such as cookies and web beacons.

Opt-out of E-mail Tracking

Although it is possible to opt-out of e-mail tracking, doing so does not come without sacrifice. Within one's individual e-mail client, one can turn off image display, disable the display of links, and decline any read-receipt requests. One should note that there are e-mail tracking services which convert the e-mail message into an image before delivering the message. One obviously cannot read the message contained in the image if image display is disabled in one's e-mail client.

HP E-mail Tracking

In the U.S. Congressional Inquiry investigating the HP pretesting scandal it was revealed that HP security used an e-mail tracking service called ReadNotify.com to investigate boardroom leaks. The California attorney general's office has said that this practice was not part of the pretesting charges. HP said they consider e-mail tracing to be legitimate and will continue using it.

E-mail Marketing

Email marketing is a form of direct marketing which uses electronic mail as a means of communicating commercial or fund-raising messages to an audience. In its broadest sense, every email sent to a potential or current customer could be considered email marketing. However, the term is usually used to refer to:

- Sending emails with the purpose of enhancing the relationship of a merchant with its current or old customers and to encourage customer loyalty and repeat business.
- Sending emails with the purpose of acquiring new customers or convincing old customers to buy something immediately.
- Adding advertisements in emails sent by other companies to their customers.
- Emails that are being sent on the Internet (Email did and does exist outside the Internet, Network Email, FIDO etc.)

Advantages of Email Marketing

Email marketing (on the Internet) is popular with companies because:

- The advantage of a mailing list is clearly the ability to distribute information to a wide range of specific, potential customers at a relatively low cost.
- Compared to other media investments such as direct mail or printed newsletters, it is less expensive.
- An exact Return on investment can be tracked ("track to basket") and has proven to be high when done properly. Email marketing is often reported as second only to search marketing as the most effective online marketing tactic.
- It is instant, as opposed to a mailed advertisement, an email arrives in a few seconds or minutes.
- It lets the advertiser "push" the message to its audience, as opposed to a website that waits for customers to come in.
- It is easy to track. An advertiser can track users via web bugs, bounce messages, un-subscribes, read-receipts, click-throughs, etc. These can be used to measure open rates, positive or negative responses, correlate sales with marketing.
- Advertisers can generate repeat business affordably and automatically
- Advertisers can reach substantial numbers of email subscribers who have opted in (consented) to receive email communications on subjects of interest to them
- Over half of Internet users check or send email on a typical day.

— Specific types of interaction with messages can trigger other messages to be automatically delivered.

— Specific types of interaction with messages can trigger other events such as updating the profile of the recipient to indicate a specific interest category.

— Green - email marketing is paper-free

Disadvantages Email marketing

Many companies use email marketing to communicate with existing customers, but many other companies send unsolicited bulk email, also known as spam.

Illicit email marketing antedates legitimate email marketing, since on the early Internet it was not permitted to use the medium for commercial purposes. As a result, marketers attempting to establish themselves as legitimate businesses in email marketing have had an uphill battle, hampered also by criminal spam operations billing themselves as legitimate.

It is frequently difficult for observers to distinguish between legitimate and spam email marketing. First off, spammers attempt to represent themselves as legitimate operators, obfuscating the issue. Second, direct-marketing political groups such as the U.S. Direct Marketing Association (DMA) have pressured legislatures to legalise activities which many Internet operators consider to be spamming, such as the sending of "opt-out" unsolicited commercial email. Third, the sheer volume of spam email has led some users to mistake legitimate commercial email (for instance, a mailing list to which the user subscribed) for spam—especially when the two have a similar appearance, as when messages include HTML and flashy graphics.

Due to the volume of spam email on the Internet, spam filters are essential to most users. Some marketers report that legitimate commercial emails frequently get caught by filters, and hidden; however, it is somewhat less common for email users to complain that spam filters block legitimate mail.

Companies considering an email marketing programme must make sure that their programme does not violate spam laws such as the United States' CAN-SPAM Act (Controlling the Assault of Non-Solicited Pornography and Marketing Act), the European Privacy & Electronic Communications Regulations 2003 or their Internet provider's acceptable use policy. Even if a company follows the law, if Internet mail administrators find that it is sending spam it is likely to be listed in blacklists such as SPEWS.

CAN-SPAM Compliance

Because the CAN-SPAM Act of 2003 authorises a USD 11,000 penalty per violation for spamming each individual recipient, many commercial email marketers within the United States utilise a service or special software that helps ensure compliance with the Act. A variety of older systems exist which do not ensure compliance with the Act. To comply with the Act's regulation of commercial email, services typically: require users to authenticate their return address and include a valid physical address, provide a one-click unsubscribe feature, and prohibit importing lists of purchased addresses which may not have given valid permission.

In addition to satisfying legal requirements, service providers stepped in to help customers to set up and manage their own email marketing campaigns. The services provide email templates, automatically handle subscriptions and removals, and generate statistics on how many messages were received and opened, and whether the recipients clicked on any links within the messages.

Opt-in Email Advertising

Opt-in email advertising or permission marketing is a method of advertising by electronic mail wherein the recipient of the advertisement has consented to receive it. It is one of several ways developed by marketers to eliminate the disadvantages of email marketing.

Email has become a very popular mode of communication across the world. It has also become extremely popular to advertise through. Some of the many advantages of advertising through email are the direct contact with the consumer and is "inexpensive, flexible, and simple to implement". There are also disadvantages attached to email advertising such as, alienating the consumer because of overload to messages or the advertisement getting deleted without getting read.

Permission email marketing may evolve into a technology that uses a handshake protocol between sender and receiver. This system is intended to eventually result in a high degree of satisfaction between consumers and marketers. If opt-in email advertising is used, the material that is emailed to consumers will be "anticipated." It is assumed that the consumer wants to receive it, which makes it unlike unsolicited advertisements sent to the consumer (often referred to as spam). Ideally, opt-in email advertisements will be more personal and relevant to the consumer than untargetted advertisements.

Bibliography

Alan Schwartz and Simson Garfinkel. Stopping Spam. O'Reilly & Associates, 1998.

Baran, Paul *On Distributed Communications.*http://www.rand.org/pubs/research_memoranda/RM3767. 1964.

Berners-Lee, Tim; Bray, Tim; Connolly, Dan; Cotton, Paul; Fielding, Roy; Jeckle, Mario; Lilley, Chris; Mendelsohn, Noah; Orchard, David; Walsh, Norman; Williams, Stuart (December 15, 2004). *Architecture of the World Wide Web, Volume One.* Version 20041215. W3C.

Bruce Schneier. *E-Mail Security : How to Keep Your Electronic Messages Private.*John Wiley & Sons, 1995.

Castells, M. *Rise of the Network Society.* 3 vols. Vol. 1. Cambridge, MA: Blackwell Publishers. 1996.

Coffman, K. G; Odlyzko, A. M. *The size and growth rate of the Internet.* AT&T Labs. http://www.dtc.umn.edu/~odlyzkc/doc/internet.size.pdf. Retrieved on 2007-05-21.

Comer, Douglas. *The Internet book.* Prentice Hall. pp. 64. 2006.

comScore. *Social Networking Explodes Worldwide as Sites Increase their Focus on Cultural Relevance.* Press release. http://www.comscore.com/press/release.asp?press=2396. Retrieved on November 9, 2008.

Csonka P. "Internet Crime; the Draft council of Europe convention on cyber-crime: A response to the challenge of crime in the age of the internet?". *Computer Law & Security Report* Vol.16 no.5.2000.

Dave Gibbons et.al., *Using E-Mail.* Que, 1994.

David Strom, Marshall T. Rose *Internet Messaging.* Harcourt Brace, 1998.

Diane B. Hartman and Karen Nantz. *The 3 Rs of E-Mail : Risks, Rights and Responsibilities*. Crisp Publications, 1996.

Dianna Booher *E-Writing: 21st Century Tools for Effective Communication*. Pocket Books, 2001.

Don Moore, Terri Kurtzberg, Leigh Thompson, and Michael Morris. *Long and Short Routes to Success in Electronically-Mediated Negotiations: Group Affiliations and Good Vibrations*.Research Paper #1484, Graduate School of Business, Stanford University.

Geoff Mulligan. *Removing the Spam: Email Processing and Filtering*. Addison-Wesley Longman, 1999.

Joan Tunstall. *Better, Faster Email: Getting the Most Out of Emai*. Allen & Unwin; April 1999.

Joan Tunstall. *Easy Email*. Allen & Unwin; 2000; ISBN 1865082945; 192 pages.

John Quarterman and Smoot Carl-Mitchell. *The E-Mail Companion: Communicating Effectively via the Internet and Other Global Networks*. Addison-Wesley, 1994.

John R. Levine. *E-Mail for Dummies*. IDG, 1997; ISBN: 0764501313; 300 pages.

Joy Van Skiver. *Simple Steps to E-Mail Success*. Wrexpress; 1998.

Lee Sproull and Sara Kiesler. *Connections : New Ways of Working in the Networked Organization*. MIT Press, 1992.

Linda Lamb. *Using Email Effectively*. O'Reilly and Associates, 1995.

Nancy Flynn and Tom Flynn. *Writing Effective E-Mail*. Crisp Publications, 1998.

Stephen A. Caswell. *E-Mail*. Artech House, 1988.

Index